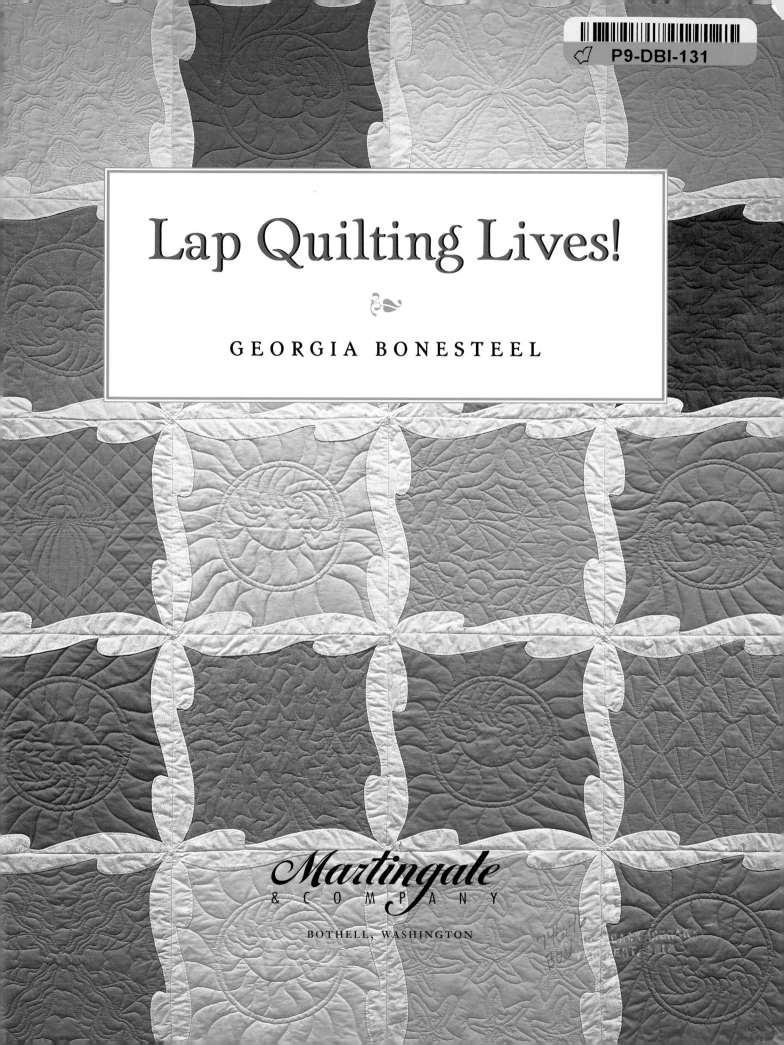

Lap Quilting Lives!

GEORGIA BONESTEEL

Martingale
& COMPANY

BOTHELL, WASHINGTON

I DEDICATE THIS BOOK TO:

Quilt teachers, whose perseverance and creativity I admire,
Pete, whose understanding may falter, but never tires,
And to my mother, who passed on the work genes that light my fire!

CREDITS

President . . . . Nancy J. Martin
CEO/Publisher . . . . .Daniel J. Martin
Associate Publisher . . . . .Jane Hamada
Editorial Director . . . . Mary V. Green
Design and Production Manager,
Cover Design . . . . Cheryl Stevenson
Technical Editor . . . . Darra Duffy Williamson
Copy Editor . . . . .Tina Cook
Illustrator . . . . Laurel Strand
Photographer . . . . Brent Kane
Designer . . . . Trina Stahl

Lap Quilting Lives!
© 1999 by Georgia J. Bonesteel

Martingale & Company
PO Box 118
Bothell, WA 98041-0118 USA
www.patchwork.com

Printed in Hong Kong
04 03 02 01 00 99   6 5 4 3 2 1

MARTINGALE & COMPANY

That Patchwork Place is an imprint of
Martingale & Company.

MISSION STATEMENT

We are dedicated to providing quality products and service by working together to inspire creativity and to enrich the lives we touch.

Library of Congress Cataloging-in-Publication Data
Bonesteel, Georgia
        Lap quilting lives! / Georgia Bonesteel
            p.   cm.
        ISBN 1-56477-259-4
        1. Patchwork Patterns.   2. Quilting Patterns.   3. Quilts.
I. Title.
TT835.B58   1999
746.46'041—dc21
                                                    99-44337
                                                    CIP

❧ Contents ❧

Introduction

ARE YOU READY to "lap it up" again?

After twenty-five years of quilting, I have come back to my quilt roots. A recent request from a symposium sponsor prompted me to teach a lap quilting class. As I prepared, I made interesting discoveries: innovative ways to connect quilted sections into a finished whole, handy methods for adapting machine quilting to the lap quilting technique, and easy ways to make reversible, "two for one" quilts.

Let me back up a moment and explain what lap quilting has meant to me over the years. When I first began to teach quilting, the class at our community college quickly found the standard frame both cumbersome and restrictive. The students had to take turns at the frame, and it appeared to me there must be a better way. My immediate stitching history was a Cajun quilting business in New Orleans. I made small hand- and machine-quilted handbags from men's necktie remnants. The typical project was perfectly sized: it fit nicely in my lap, was portable and easy to handle, and could be quilted in a reasonable amount of time.

By combining my previous sewing experience with the needs of that first quilting class, I discovered my craft calling—lap quilting. It has led to ten public television series and many books, workshops, and conventions. The end product—a finished quilt—is always the goal, with teacher-student contact being my continual inspiration.

Lap quilting can be accomplished in two ways: by piecing, appliquéing, and quilting individual sections and *then* joining the sections to form a single, larger quilt; or by making an entire quilt top and then quilting it "in the lap," from the center, one area at a time.

Many of today's quiltmakers entered the quilt world through the former, piece-by-piece approach to lap quilting. The appeal was breaking the project into simple, manageable steps, rather than trying to tackle the whole expanse at once.

You might have some UFO's (unfinished objects) in your closets today. Now is the time to rescue those projects and try my updated approach to quilt assembly. In *Lap Quilting Lives*, I dispel the notion of lap quilting as being limited to small blocks or units. You'll discover an array of exciting new quilts: some tried-and-true renditions adapted to quilt-as-you-go methods, some unique styles that combine hand and machine quilting, and some "just gotta make" treats. You'll find that the fabric you choose for the backing will be just as important as the fabric you choose for the front, not only as a background to highlight your stitches or disguise joining seams, but also as a vehicle for fun and creativity, an opportunity to design a second quilt "top."

I have always tried to meet the challenge of adapting and passing on quilt patterns for our times. That commitment includes taking advantage of new tools, up-to-date techniques, and beautiful fabrics. Many of the quilts included here are featured in my tenth television series, "Coast to Coast Lap Quilting." Every quilt has its own life, its reason for creation. Sharing these stories brings a focus to the quilt and gives the maker (and the owner!) a better understanding of its history. I invite you to stitch away with me . . . and stay warm in style.

A Quilter's Vocabulary

"Prune the dog ears for the block assembly."

Yes, we quilters have our own language, one that has evolved over the years. Add the following definitions to your quilt vocabulary for a keen understanding of our craft.

Appliqué: From the French word *appliquér*, meaning to put or lay on. In stitchery, appliqué refers to shapes or figures that have been cut out, then sewn to a larger piece of foundation material. The application can be made in several ways. Raw edges can be basted under in advance or needleturned, then secured with a hidden slipstitch or with a running stitch. Appliqués can also be applied with a hand or machine buttonhole stitch, or with the satin stitch or blind hemstitch on your sewing machine.

Backing: The bottom or back layer of a quilt, also called the *lining*. Preshrinking is advised. Avoid taffeta or other slippery fabric for backings. Muslin is the most popular backing, but small-scale prints work well for lap quilting since they help disguise the seams where blocks or units are joined.

> ❧ *Avoid an obvious center seam in your pieced quilt backs. Begin with a large center panel, then add equally sized strips to either side for a nice, professional finish.*

Basting: A long, temporary running stitch used to secure the three layers (top, batting, and backing) of the quilt "sandwich" prior to machine or hand quilting. For best results, start in the center of the project and work outward, basting about every six to seven inches for a large quilt. Use contrasting thread (so it's easy to see), and keep knots visible so they are easy to remove when the quilting is done.

Bias: The diagonal of the fabric, which has the most give and stretch. The bias runs at a 45-degree angle to its lengthwise and crosswise threads. Narrow strips are often cut along the bias to use as quilt binding.

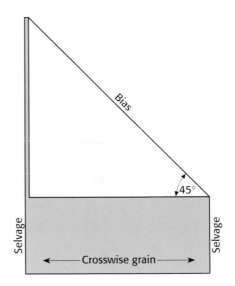

Binding: A narrow strip of folded fabric sewn to the outer raw edges of a completed quilt. Binding can be cut on the lengthwise or crosswise straight of grain, or on the bias.

Block: A unit of patchwork or appliqué, most often square, that is repeated to construct a quilt top.

Borders: Strips or panels intended to frame (or partially frame) a large area of a quilt or an entire quilt. Borders can be whole cloth, pieced, appliquéd, or made with any combination of fabrics and techniques. The corners can be mitered, butted, or finished with squares in a contrasting color.

Catywhompus: When the top and bottom layers of a quilt shift or are askew, we sometimes say that "things are catywhompus" or that "catywhompus has happened!"

Corner square: Small fabric squares sometimes inserted at sashing intersections.

Cross-hatching: Straight-line quilting done in an overall pattern of intersecting perpendicular (right-angle) lines. The lines can be either vertical and horizontal or diagonal.

Diagonal cross-hatching

Dangling thread: A length of thread literally left dangling when lines of quilting are interrupted prior to the joining of lap-quilted units. Once the units are joined, the "dangles" are re-threaded and the quilting completed.

Dog ears: Triangular extensions formed when diagonal pieces are sewn together. Dog ears should be "pruned," or snipped off, to reduce bulk before piecing continues.

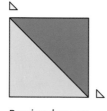

Pruning dog ears

Echo quilting: Radiating quilting that outlines or mimics a pieced or appliquéd shape.

Foolproof knot: In 1979—more than twenty years ago!—I introduced this knot on my first television show, and it amazes me how it has spread through the quilt community. I learned it at a quilt symposium from a person who had just seen it at a lecture. It makes a tidy replacement for the "dirty finger twirl" we often make for hand sewing.

I use this dependable knot for hand piecing, appliqué, and quilting. It's made by wrapping a single thread around the needle (like creating a French knot), and then sliding the knot down the length of the thread.

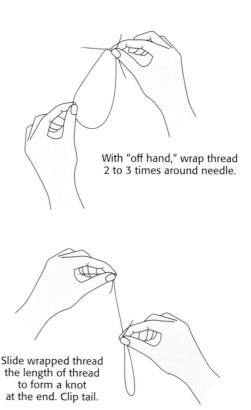

Hold threaded needle parallel
to your body; grasp the thread end
between your thumb and forefinger.

With "off hand," wrap thread
2 to 3 times around needle.

Slide wrapped thread
the length of thread
to form a knot
at the end. Clip tail.

Fudging: Making things work when they are not quite perfect! In patchwork, fudging usually refers to manipulating fabric to make slightly mismatched pieces fit, such as at misaligned seam intersections.

Grain line: A reference to the warp threads (the taut threads running parallel to the selvage) and the woof threads (the stretchier threads running crosswise from selvage to selvage) that are woven together to form fabric (see "Bias" on page 5).

Half-square triangle: A right-angle triangle which, when joined to another along its matching bias edge, forms a square.

Half-Square Triangle

In-the-ditch: A line of quilting done in the depression created by a seam, on the side of the seam that is free from the seam allowance.

Lap quilting: To quilt in blocks or units, afterward joining the quilted sections to form an entire quilt. Quilting may be done with or without a hoop or lap frame. *Lap quilting* also refers to quilting a complete quilt top "in the lap"—or in any manner other than in a floor frame.

Marking: The process of transferring designs onto the quilt top as a guide for quilting. Marking should be done lightly, and be either removable or invisible when quilting is complete (see "Marking Tools" on page 11).

Meander quilting: Random squiggly quilting lines made by hand or machine. Sometimes referred to as *stippling*, and often used as filler or background in a single block or entire quilt.

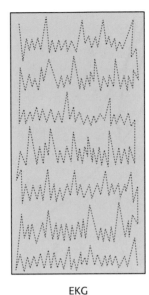

Squiggles

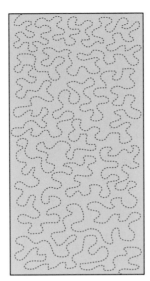

EKG

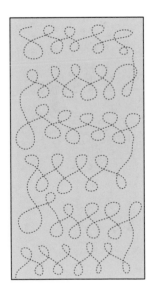

Stars

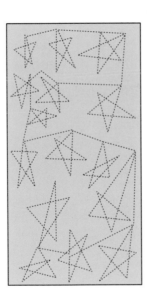

Lazy Eights

Miter: A right-angle (45-degree), diagonal seam at the corner of a block or border.

Notions: The tools of our trade! The paraphernalia and gizmos used to make quilts, such as thread, needles, scissors, and thimbles.

Off hand: The hand that works under the quilt during the quilting process, ensuring that all the layers have been pierced. Ideally, a suitable covering protects the finger that guides the needle back to the quilt top. Possibilities include a thimble, a layer of masking tape, a coating of clear nail polish, the finger of an old glove, or any number of state-of-the-art notions.

On-point: A block rotated 45 degrees is said to be "set on-point."

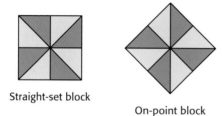

Straight-set block

On-point block

Patchwork: The art of building a large piece of decorative cloth from smaller pieces. Could be renamed "patchfun."

Piecing or piecework: The process of sewing two or more pieces of fabric together with a sewing machine or by hand, using a small running stitch, coordinating thread, and a ¼" seam allowance.

> ❧ *Achieve neat and secure hand-stitched seams by making a backstitch after every five or six stitches.*

Prune: To trim excess fabric or triangular points to even the edges of a block (see "Dog ears" on page 6).

Quarter-square triangle: When a square is divided on both diagonals, each of the four resulting right-angle triangles is called a quarter-square triangle.

Quarter-square triangle

Quilt sandwich: The three layers of a typical quilt: quilt top, batting, and backing.

Row assembly: The process of creating and joining vertical or horizontal rows from lap-quilted blocks, units, or panels.

Sampler quilt: A quilt comprised of various blocks made with different patterns and techniques. Blocks may be the same size or various sizes.

Sashing: Sometimes called *lattice*, these narrow strips of fabric are sewn between blocks to frame or otherwise highlight them.

Scrappy quilt: A quilt made up of a wide variety of different fabrics, usually leftover scraps.

Setting: The arrangement of individual blocks or units to create an overall design. Settings can be straight or diagonal, done with or without sashing, and so on.

Stencil: Designs cut in paper or vinyl and marked on the quilt top as a guide for quilting.

Template: A pattern made from durable material (cardboard, plastic, sandpaper, Grid-Grip, or vinyl) and used to transfer shapes onto fabric. Accurate templates are a key factor in precision piecework, ensuring uniformity in size and shape.

Tied quilt: A quilt sandwich fastened at regular intervals with knots of embroidery floss or yarn rather than with quilting stitches.

The Right Stuff

As I tidy up after a day at my sewing machine, I sometimes ponder the "right stuff"—all the materials and notions we quilters rely on to make a quilt. Truthfully, all we really require is fabric, something to cut it apart with, and something we can use to put it back together again to create a new design. But nowadays there are many wonderful tools to help us make those tasks more efficient and fun.

Being a list maker, let me present an itemized account of the quiltmaking supplies I like to have on hand, starting with the essentials:

Fabric: The raw material for making quilt tops and backings. One hundred percent cotton in solid colors and prints (including flannels and woven checks and plaids) is the preferred fabric for full-size quilts, while decorative wall hangings (which don't receive as much wear) allow for experimenting with synthetics, glitzy fabrics, and other unusual textures.

As a rule, I avoid tightly woven, difficult-to-needle materials (such as percale sheets); loosely woven or gauzy fabrics that allow batting to poke through the quilt top; heavyweight fabrics that create extra-bulky seam connections; and nap fabrics that hide quilting stitches.

Batting: The filler, or insulating middle layer, of a quilt. Batting comes in various thicknesses and fibers—polyester, cotton, wool, silk, and blends. You can find it packaged in a variety of sizes, or on the roll for purchase by the yard.

Sewing machine: No fudging here! I recommend that you treat yourself to the best you can afford: you and your quilts deserve it. While a good, dependable running stitch is all that is necessary, an adjustable satin stitch, a blind hemstitch, and a decorative buttonhole stitch are popular—and useful—for today's quiltmaking techniques. Not necessary but nice to have is a patchwork presser foot, the edge of which measures a precise ¼" from the needle, to aid piecing accuracy.

Patchwork foot

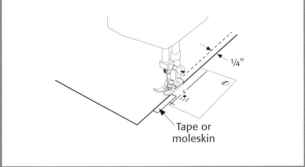

❧ *If you don't have—or can't find—a patchwork foot for your sewing machine, you can still create a guide for accurate seam allowances. Carefully place a strip of masking tape or moleskin (available at your local pharmacy) on the throat plate, exactly ¼" from the needle.*

¼"

Tape or moleskin

Thread: Keep a supply of good-quality, neutral-colored (white, beige, gray, black) thread in cotton and cotton-wrapped polyester for hand and machine piecework, plus variously colored quilting threads in cotton and wax-coated cotton. (Quilting thread is too thick for piecework at the sewing machine.) It's also nice to have decorative rayon, silk, and metallic threads for adding shimmery accents.

Embroidery floss: This is cotton, rayon, or silk floss used for embellishment on appliqué and crazy patch blocks. It is usually stitched in multiple strands with a special embroidery needle.

Needles: For machine stitching, I recommend #80 as an all-purpose needle for sewing cotton fabrics. A #90 is perfect for handling denim and other heavyweight fabrics, while the finer #70 works well for lighter weights. Notice that the higher the needle's number, the thicker and heavier the fabric it can handle.

A Metafil needle—a special needle with an extended eye—nicely accommodates all the metallic and rayon threads, while a 4.0 double needle is extremely useful for stitching narrow, fusible bias trim.

Hand-quilting needles, also called Betweens, come in a variety of sizes, from #3 to #12. (With hand-quilting needles, the higher the number, the smaller and finer the needle.) I prefer a #12, which makes a fine quilting stitch, but I suggest you experiment to find your favorite size.

Select appliqué needles that are long and fine for ease in turning raw edges and manipulating tiny pieces. I use needles called Sharps, #11 or #12, for both appliqué and hand piecing. You might also want to try the curved needles that are available for hand basting.

Machine needles can become dull and burred and should be replaced after twelve to twenty-four hours of sewing. Keep a log near your machine and record each needle replacement, just as you would when replacing oil in your car. By the way, those old machine needles make great nails for hanging lightweight objects on the wall!

Scissors: Sharpened, for-fabric-only shears are a must. For trimming appliqués and other specialty work, I keep a pair of "lip" scissors (the pelican-bill variety) and small, pointed embroidery scissors. Use paper or utility scissors to cut templates and freezer paper, and keep a tiny pair of thread clippers handy.

Rotary cutters, mats, and rulers: Rotary cutters and their accessories (self-healing cutting mats and acrylic rulers) have become almost indispensable to today's quiltmaker. These tools are available in many sizes and designs. You'll want to experiment to find the ones that suit you best.

My personal brand preference for rulers is Omnigrid. These sturdy, $\frac{1}{8}$"-gridded rulers are versatile, accurate, and easy to read.

Pins: Long, large-headed quilter's pins are great for basting and other utilitarian stitching tasks. Silk pins, which are small and fine with tiny heads, are ideal for appliqué. Throw away any pin when it becomes dull or burred. You don't want to ruin your precious fabrics!

Marking tools: Common marking tools include water-soluble fabric markers; chalk wedges, pencils, and rollers; silver and white pencils; and soap slivers. Never use a ballpoint pen or any other permanent marker to mark quilting lines.

Sometimes you can avoid marking altogether by quilting around pre-cut, reusable Con-Tact paper patterns, or along the edges of masking tape.

> ❧ *Always test your marking device before using it to mark your quilt! You'll want to be certain it is easy to remove when the quilting is complete.*

Thimbles: If you stitch by hand, you'll want one of these, especially for hand quilting. Thimbles come in all shapes, sizes, and materials—from silver to leather to plastic. I prefer a silver thimble with an indented rim around the closed end and a ridge at the open end, which helps me control the needle.

Hoops: I like narrow 6" and 9" hoops for machine quilting, and supported lap hoops for hand quilting in my lap.

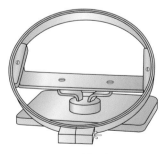

Supported lap hoop

Template material: Possibilities include cardboard, plastic (or vinyl) sheets—including the heat-resistant variety for pressing appliqué seam allowances—and freezer paper. I use Grid-Grip, a special gridded freezer paper I've developed just for patchwork (see "Resources" on page 110).

Flexicurve, or flexible curve: These bendable tubes can be shaped to mark fabric for curved piecing or appliqué placement. They come in a variety of lengths; I prefer 18".

Flexible curve

Walking foot: This handy foot helps you feed the three layers of a quilt sandwich evenly under the presser foot of your sewing machine to prevent "catywhompus." It is perfect for straight-line quilting, and even works for quilting gentle curves.

Walking foot

Seam ripper: Need I say more?

Miscellaneous notions: Nonessential but handy notions to have on hand include a glue-stick for a variety of sewing-room tasks, a calculator for figuring yardage and measurements, a stiletto to guide fabric pieces smoothly under the sewing-machine presser foot, and bias bars for making continuous bias strips for appliqué.

❧ Quilting Variations ❧

It used to be that a quilt was not a quilt unless it was made totally by hand. Wow, have we come a long way! Along with new ways to quilt—including by machine—we have developed new ways to hold the layered quilt while hand quilting, either with or without a hoop or lap frame.

In lap quilting, the quilting typically is done in units, before the entire quilt top is connected. Here are some things to consider before you begin quilting:

What should I quilt?

Consider the shadows and texture the quilting stitches bring to your finished quilt, lending warmth and beauty. Rather than an afterthought, think of the quilting as another element of the quilt's design. I begin thinking about the quilting designs as I construct the quilt top. Should the lines be soft and fluid or straight and geometric? Should they follow and outline the piecing or appliqué or should they create a secondary pattern on the quilt?

How should I transfer the quilting designs to the quilt top?

The quilting design is usually transferred before the quilt sandwich is basted. You might choose to trace pre-cut stencils or printed patterns from books or magazines. Other options include creating your own designs with cookie cutters, rulers, masking tape, Con-Tact paper, a flexicurve, dinner plates, or a teacup. See "Marking tools" on page 11 for suggestions on suitable markers.

Lap quilting in sections requires that you plan ahead. Leave an unquilted margin of at least ½" along edges where units will be joined.

> ❧ *You'll find it easier to trace patterns from a book or magazine if you layer the pattern and quilt block over a light source. Try a light box, or tape your block to a sunny window.*

What type of batting should I use?

When it comes to batting you have lots of choices, and all have a different drape, weight, and feel (see "Batting" on page 9). Some battings are easier to needle than others. Experiment with several brands to find the one that gives your quilt the desired character. Other things to consider: How much quilting do you plan to do? Will you quilt by hand, machine, or both? How will the finished quilt be used and how often will it need to be laundered?

What color should I use for quilting thread?

More decisions! You can elect to use the same thread color throughout or you can combine a variety of colors, depending on the effect you're looking for. Keep the fabric color in mind—both front and back. High-contrast thread will show off your quilting stitches, while low-contrast thread will keep stitches in the background. Many a beginning quilter would hesitate to quilt with white thread on a navy blue backing!

Hoopless Hand Quilting

SOMEONE once told me that I was not quilting because I was not using a frame. Of course I was: I was still connecting three layers with small running stitches. In fact, I know some wonderful quilters who take excellent quilting stitches on full-size quilts and never use a hoop!

Once the three layers are basted, quilting can begin. Start in the center of a block, panel, row, or other small unit. Make a foolproof knot (page 6) in an 18" to 24" length of quilting thread and bury it by "popping" it into the quilt top.

When I hand quilt, my off hand holds the layers under the quilt and acts as a feeder for the needle hand. I hold the needle parallel to my body and take three to five running stitches on my needle at a time. The ridge around the open end of my thimble acts as a pusher, protecting my finger and helping the needle to go through the layers.

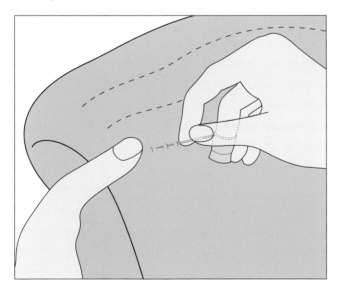

You can avoid starting with a knotted thread altogether. Begin in the middle of a line or design—one in which you can quilt out in two directions. Thread the needle with an extra-long piece of unknotted thread. Pull the thread halfway into the layers, leaving the other half to dangle. Quilt to the end of the thread and tie off with a hidden knot, then rethread the needle with the dangling tail and quilt in the opposite direction.

Hoop or Frame Hand Quilting

For large basted units or panels, or for complete quilt tops, a 16" or 18" hoop works well. The advantage of a hoop is that the quilt can be turned and the needle hand does not end up in an awkward position.

Place the center of the basted quilt in the hoop and adjust the tension. Don't make it too tight or there will not be enough give in the quilt for you to maneuver the needle. As each area is completed, remove the hoop and move it to a new section of the basted quilt for quilting.

Try stitching with a rocking motion. Use a thimble that has a well or indention at the end for positioning and controlling the needle (see "Thimbles" on page 11). Insert the needle into the quilt top at a right angle, and position the thimble finger over the needle. With the thumb out ahead, use the thimble to gently push the needle up and down. Quilt toward yourself, taking three to five stitches on the needle before pulling it through. The thumb, resting on the quilt surface ahead of the needle, gauges the length of each stitch.

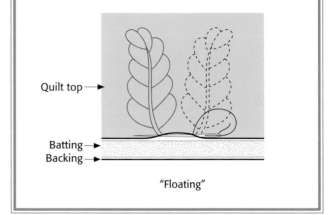

<svg>✒</svg> *When you have only a short distance to travel from the end of one quilting line to the beginning of another, slide the needle through the layers to "float" to the next starting point. Every knot is a vulnerable spot on your quilt—knots can pull out with time and wear—so the fewer stops and starts, the better.*

"Floating"

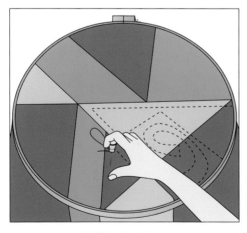

Quilting in a hoop

Machine Quilting

WHILE it can be cumbersome and tiring to quilt a full-size quilt by machine, quilting in sections on the sewing machine is both sensible and manageable. Why not give it a try?

Think of your sewing machine as an extension of your hands. Treat it with tender, loving care—give it proper oiling and cleaning and change the needles regularly.

Don't be swept up by the notion that machine quilting is so fast and easy it will allow you to move quickly on to new projects. Not so! Be prepared to dedicate as many hours at the machine as you spent learning to hand quilt. My best advice: practice, practice . . . and practice! Start with small projects, take classes, and experiment to find what is best for you. Over time, you'll probably develop your own machine-quilting style.

> ⨭ *You'll want as few stops and starts as possible when machine quilting. Look for designs that can be quilted in long, continuous lines.*

MEANDERING

Dropping the feed dogs on your sewing machine allows you to quilt in any direction without maneuvering harsh angles. I use a clear plastic, freehand quilting foot that allows good visibility as I stitch. I also favor a narrow 9" wooden hoop, with the outer hoop under the backing, and the inner hoop snapped in position over the area to be quilted. The hoop holds the layers taut and gives me something to hold on to as I maneuver. (Some quilters meander without a hoop, but it takes strong hands!)

Take one stitch to start, pull the bobbin thread through to the top of the quilt, and stitch in place to lock the threads. Stop after a few stitches, and snip the beginning thread tails. Start meandering by "doodling" over the desired area (see page 7). Practice on floral fabric, following the curves of the flower motifs, until you can maintain an even ten to twelve stitches per inch.

When the hoop area is filled with quilting, lower the needle into the fabric, release the hoop, and move it to the next area to be quilted.

COMBINATION HAND AND MACHINE QUILTING

Combining machine and hand quilting on the same quilt is becoming more and more popular. The techniques complement each other, with each acting as a stabilizer for the other.

Different situations lend themselves to different methods. For example, you'll probably want to hand quilt on solid fabrics where stitches are more visible, but machine quilt on busy prints where hand quilting tends to get lost. Save stencils and quilting patterns with lots of fancy stops and starts for hand quilting, and focus on continuous-line designs for quilting by machine. Another way to combine techniques is to machine quilt in-the-ditch (see page 7) to anchor blocks, panels, or rows before adding fancy hand-quilted designs.

> ⨭ *Some consider it old-fashioned, but one step of the quilting process I never skip is thread basting. I find it essential to carefully stabilize the layers before I quilt by hand or machine.*

ৰু Lap Quilting Connections ৯৯

It's easy to build a full-size quilt by joining smaller, already-quilted blocks or rows. Just follow these simple instructions.

Block to Block

Once the individual blocks are quilted, you are ready to join the blocks into rows.

1. Remove basting threads, masking tape, and quilt markings, then trim all sides of each block so that the edges of the top, batting, and backing are even.

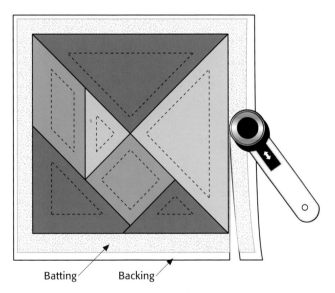

Batting   Backing

2. Select 2 adjacent blocks. Pin back the backing and batting on 1 block along the edge to be joined. For the second block, pin back only the backing along the edge to be joined.

3. Place the blocks right sides together, aligning the edges you just pinned. Pin the blocks together for sewing, matching the block ends and centers first, then easing as necessary.

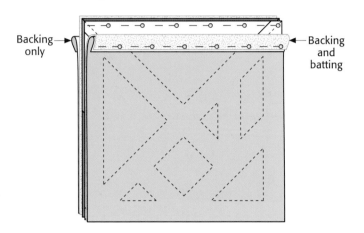

Backing only → ← Backing and batting

4. Position the pinned blocks at your sewing machine so that the block with both the batting and batting folded back is on top. Using a ¼" seam allowance, sew the blocks together. You will catch the batting from the bottom block in the seam.

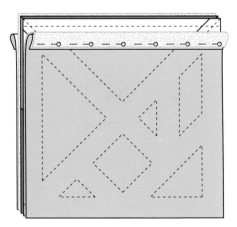

5. Repeat steps 1–4 until each row is complete. Remove all the pins, and place 1 stitched row face down on a flat surface. The seam with the stitched batting will fall flat. Trim the loose batting from the other block so that it butts up to the seamed batting. Any batting that overlaps will create bulk.

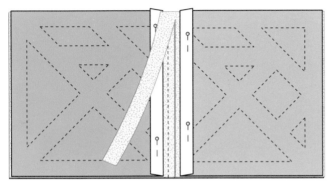

Trim batting ¼" to butt against seam.

6. Smooth 1 flap of backing fabric flat, and turn the other flap under ¼" to form a flat lapped seam. (Sometimes this lapped side can be basted ahead of time as in the wave backing on "Heart to Heart" on page 26.) Finish the seam with a hand appliqué stitch or slipstitch in matching thread. Be careful not to stitch through to the front.

7. Sew the rows together, using the same technique you used to join the blocks. Pin carefully to match seams, and snip batting at intersections as necessary. Be sure to work on a flat surface to avoid puckers.

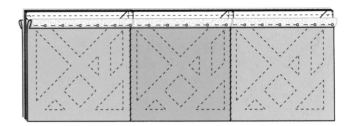

Row to Row

LAP quilting works well when blocks can be pre-assembled into vertical or horizontal rows, and then basted and quilted before being joined to form the quilt top. This technique eliminates block-to-block stitching and allows you to work with larger, but still manageable, units during the quilting stage.

1. Remove basting threads, masking tape, and quilt markings, then trim all sides of each row so that the edges of the top, batting, and backing are even.

2. Select 2 adjacent rows. On 1 row only, trim the batting an additional ¼" along the edge to be joined.

3. Place the rows right sides together. Along the edge to be joined, pin together all but 1 layer. (The unpinned layer can be either the quilt top or backing.) Pin the free layer back so that it will be out of the way when you stitch the rows together.

4. Position the pinned row at your sewing machine so that the side with the trimmed batting lies against the feed dogs. Machine stitch, using a ¼" seam allowance.

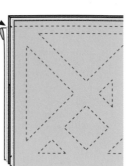

Batting trimmed additional ¼"

5. Starting in the center of the row, turn under the free fabric layer ¼" to form a flat, lapped seam. Finish the seam with a hand appliqué stitch or slipstitch in matching thread. Be careful not to stitch through to the front.

Accent-Binding Connection

Bringing color and patchwork to the back of a quilt leads us to another form of lap quilting. With an accent-binding connection, you can quilt all the way to the connecting edge of the block or row rather than leaving the usual ½"-wide unquilted margins.

1. When basting the 3 layers of the quilt, trim the batting ¼" short of the raw edges where the connections will be made. This uneven layering allows you to quilt to the outer edges and reduces bulk.

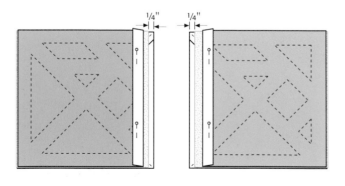

2. Align the edges of 2 adjacent panels. Position 1 edge of a separate accent or patchwork strip face down along the raw edge of the back of 1 panel as shown, and pin. You will be stitching through 5 layers: the front and back of each quilt panel, and the accent strip.

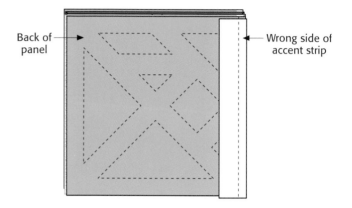

Back of panel

Wrong side of accent strip

3. Place the quilt on a flat surface, and fold the accent strip over the raw edges of the seam to form a ¼" seam allowance. Pin in place and hand stitch, taking care not to go through to the front side. As an alternative, if you are comfortable with your bobbin thread showing, you might try a decorative machine stitch—visible on both quilt top and backing—to finish the seam.

When using the accent-binding connection, it's best to stagger the blocks from row to row, the way bricks are staggered in a wall. You'll avoid lots of excess bulk at the connections.

Tried and True

Ah, tradition. We love the old familiar designs,
but how wonderful to update the construction methods!
With these tried-and-true projects, we'll explore classic appliqué
and pieced designs that adapt easily to sectional construction.

Heart to Heart

A circa 1850 wedding quilt from the collection of the Museum of Early Southern Decorative Arts in Winston-Salem, North Carolina, became the springboard for an intriguing craft/art challenge. I took on the challenge and made three different heart quilts, plus an entire heart-themed ensemble. The heart pattern included here is glorious in bright oranges, reds, and yellows, and it combines both hand and machine quilting. The blocks are joined in rows, then quilted for a row-to-row lap-quilted connection.

Finished Block Size: 12"

Materials

(44"-WIDE FABRIC)

- 1½ yds. *each* of 2 contrasting pastels for background blocks
- 1⅛ yds. contrasting stripe for middle border and corner squares
- 1⅛ yds. light pastel for inner border
- 2 yds. multicolored print for sashing
- ⅔ yd. bright fabric for outer border (can be 1 of the heart fabrics)
- 20 different bright squares, each 12" x 12", for the hearts
- 5 different panels, each 24" x 84", for the backing
- 36" x 36" square of fabric for binding
- Queen-size batting (90" x 108")

Cutting

All measurements include ¼"-wide seam allowances.

From *each* of the 2 contrasting pastels for background blocks, cut:

- 10 squares, each 12⅞" x 12⅞"

From the contrasting stripe, cut:

- 9 strips, each 2" x 42", for the middle borders
- 30 squares, each 4¾" x 4¾", for the corner squares

From the light pastel border fabric, cut:

- 9 strips, each 4" x 42", for the inner borders

From the multicolored print, cut:

- 49 rectangles, each 4" x 12½", for the sashing

From the bright outer-border fabric, cut:

- 9 strips, each 2½" x 42"

From the 5 backing panels, cut:

- 1 rectangle, 20" x 84", for row 3
- 2 rectangles, each 20" x 84", for rows 2 and 4 *(Reserve the remaining 2 panels for rows 1 and 5)*

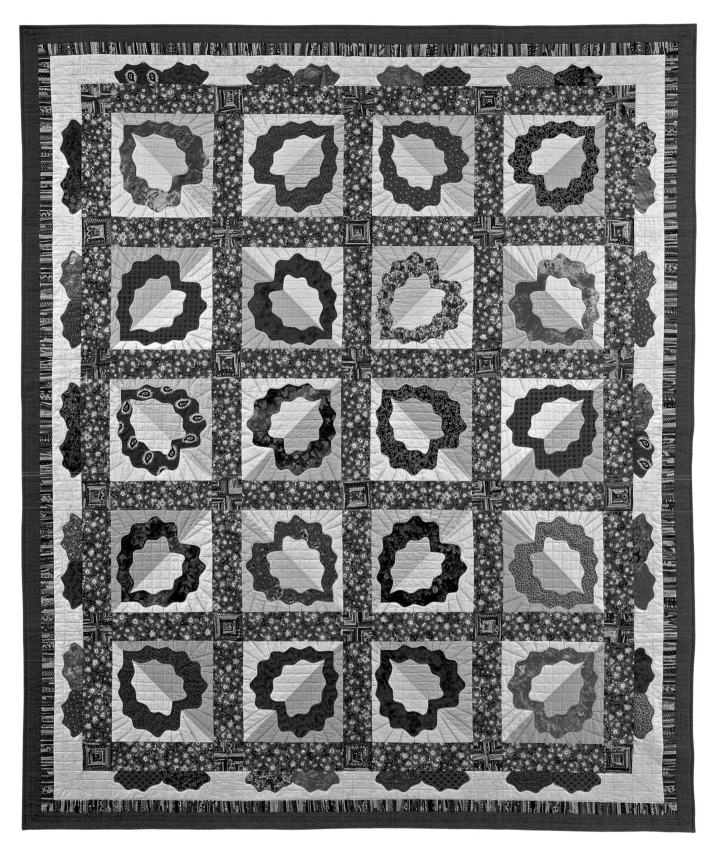

Heart to Heart, 79½" x 95", by Georgia J. Bonesteel, quilted by Georgia J. Bonesteel,
Genevieve Grundy, and Velma Everhart.

Quilt back

Piecing the Heart Blocks

1. Place 2 of the 12⅞" pastel squares—1 of each color—right sides together. Use a see-through gridded ruler to mark the top square in half along 1 diagonal.

2. Mark a line ¼" from each side of the diagonal line. Machine stitch directly on the 2 new lines.

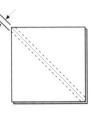

3. Use a rotary cutter or scissors to cut on the original diagonal line.

4. Open the 2 triangles, and press the seam toward the darker fabric. Trim the dog ears.

Make 20.

5. Repeat steps 1–4 to make 20 half-square triangle units.

Appliquéing the Hearts

1. Make a template from the heart pattern on the pull-out. Fold each of the twenty 12" squares in half right side out, and trace the template on the fold as shown. Cut out the hearts, adding ¼" seam allowances to the fabric shapes as you cut.

Template

2. Cut the smaller, inside hearts in half lengthwise.

Cut.

3. Place 2 different heart halves right sides together, mark a crosswise stitching line as shown, and stitch. Trim, leaving a ¼" seam allowance, and set the pieced cutaways aside to use as border accents.

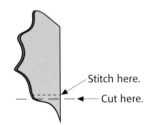

Stitch here.

Cut here.

4. Pin a large, intact heart to each background square, aligning the midpoint of the heart with the diagonal seam of the block. Appliqué as desired.

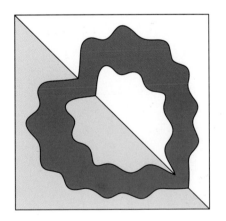

I appliquéd my hearts by machine. After snipping the concave curves to make turning easier, I folded and pressed the raw edges over heat-resistant templates cut to match the finished heart. To stitch, I used transparent nylon thread and a blind hemstitch, with the needle positioned close to the turned-under edge.

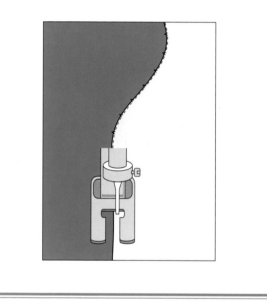

Adding the Setting Squares and Sashing

1. Cut each 4¾" striped square twice diagonally to form quarter-square triangles. Switch 2 triangles in each square as shown, and stitch to reassemble the squares.

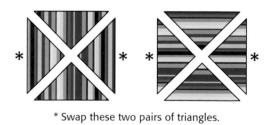

* Swap these two pairs of triangles.

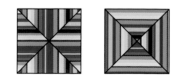

2. To form row 1, lay out 9 sashing strips, 5 corner squares, and 4 heart blocks as shown in the quilt diagram on page 25. Repeat to form rows 2, 4, and 5. Refer to the photo on page 21 for guidance in properly positioning the heart blocks. For row 3, lay out the remaining 13 sashing strips, 10 corner squares, and 4 heart blocks. Assemble the rows, but don't join them.

Making and Attaching the Borders

1. Piece the 4"-wide pastel border strips into 1 continuous 4"-wide strip. Sew the joining seams diagonally (see the tip box below). Repeat to make continuous strips from the 2"-wide striped border strips, and from the 2½"-wide bright border strips.

For easy diagonal piecing, stack border strips of matching width right side up. Use your rotary cutter and ruler to cut a 45-degree angle at each end of the stacked strips, then swing every other strip around for piecing, as shown.

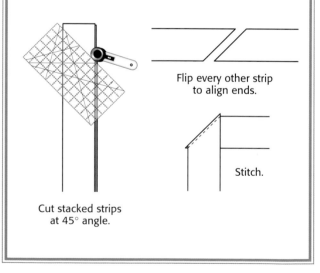

Flip every other strip to align ends.

Stitch.

Cut stacked strips at 45° angle.

2. To form a single border unit, sew the 3 strips together along their long edges in the order shown, and press. Cut the border unit into the following segments:

- 2 strips, each 7½" x 80", for top and bottom borders
- 4 strips, each 7½" x 23", for row 1 and row 5 side borders
- 4 strips, each 7½" x 16", for row 2 and row 4 side borders
- 2 strips, each 7½" x 19½", for row 3 side borders

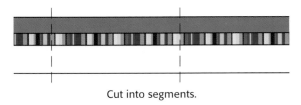

Cut into segments.

3. Position each side-border segment beside the appropriate row. Place a pieced half-heart on the inner border beside each block, aligning the seam with the center of the block, not the row. Refer to the quilt diagram and to the photo on page 21 for guidance. Pin the pieced cutaways to the border segments, then use your preferred method to appliqué the hearts in place—I used a machine satin stitch. Repeat to position and appliqué 4 pieced cutaways to both the top and bottom borders.

4. Place the side-border segments and the top and bottom borders around the sashed rows. Pin, then stitch the borders in place, mitering the corners on rows 1 and 5. Do not join the rows yet; we'll do that after the rows are quilted.

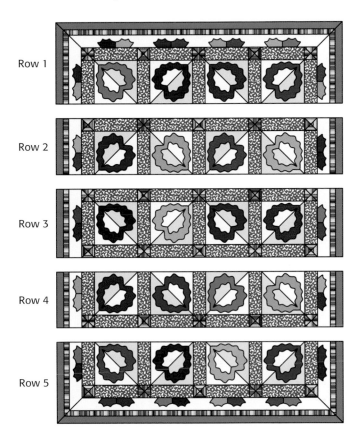

Row 1

Row 2

Row 3

Row 4

Row 5

Quilting and Finishing

1. Fold the backing panels for rows 2 and 4 in half so that the long edges meet. Use a flexicurve (page 11) to mark gentle waves along the long raw edges, then cut along the marked lines. Baste under a ¼" seam allowance along each wavy raw edge. Layer each row with the batting and appropriate backing panels, then baste.

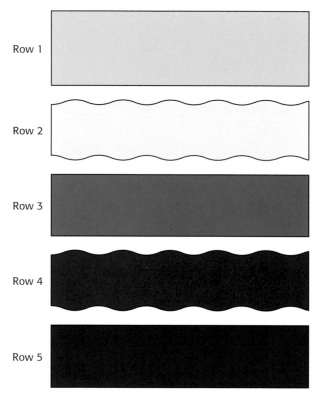

Backing panels

2. Quilt as desired, leaving at least ½" unquilted at the panel edges. In the sample quilt, hand-quilted cross-hatching fills the interior of each heart, and machine novelty stitches radiate outward.

3. Join the rows, using the row-to-row construction method (page 17). To finish the back, hand stitch the basted wavy edges in place, being careful not to stitch through to the front. Finish quilting the sashing and borders after the rows are joined.

4. Cut the 36" square of binding fabric into 2½"-wide strips. The fabric is sufficient for cutting on the straight of grain or on the bias, whichever you prefer. Bind the quilt to finish.

The heart motif took on special significance during the creation of this quilt. Our family lost a beautiful granddaughter, Maggie Wyn Bonesteel, to Spinal Muscular Atrophy (SMA) after seven months of life. At her christening, my daughter Amy turned to me, saying, "I could feel every heart in that room break." So I adapted the Heart to Heart pattern to include a break on two sides. The positive-negative heart block is set on-point with large triangles of contrasting color.

I met Sandy Bonsib around this time and became intrigued with her photo-transfer methods (see "Resources" on page 110). It seemed the perfect touch to use photo transfers of Maggie for her initials and the date.

Broken Heart Wall Hanging, 23" x 23", by Georgia J. Bonesteel.

Pieced Pastel Pleasures

One day, a brown paper bag appeared in my office with a note attached. The note read: "I have no use for this quilt top, maybe you do." Upon looking inside, I discovered a pastel pleasure of elongated hexagons. Once it had been quilted for me by Marie Detwiler, it found a home on my guest bed, where it brightened a dark paneled room.

Sometime later, I needed a project for my yearly Freedom Escape classes in Weaverville, North Carolina, and took a closer look at this old-fashioned, elongated hexagon pattern. I remade the quilt and developed quick-piecing methods to hasten the process. Afterward I was even more in awe of the anonymous quilter who set in those lavender squares!

When making "Pieced Pastel Pleasures," your first task is to collect fabric for the hexagon combinations. If you want a scrap look, try exchanging rectangles with friends.

Materials
(44"-WIDE FABRIC)

- 3 yds. light blue solid for inner border, A squares, and B triangles
- 2⅛ yds. lavender solid for B and E triangles
- 1 yd. *total* of assorted scraps for C and D triangles
- 1½ yds. light pastel print for outer border
- 152 assorted rectangles, each 5" x 7½", for elongated hexagons
- 9 yds. fabric for backing
- 32" x 32" square of fabric for binding
- Queen-size batting (90" x 108")

Cutting

All measurements include ¼"-wide seam allowances.

From the light blue solid, cut:

- 2 strips, each 2" x 88½", for the side inner borders
- 4 strips, each 2" x 26⅜", for the top and bottom inner borders (panels 1 and 3)
- 2 strips, each 2" x 24⅞", for the top and bottom inner borders (panel 2)
- 63 squares, each 5⅜" x 5⅜", for the A squares
- 32 squares, each 6⅛" x 6⅛", for the B triangles

From the lavender solid, cut:

- 60 squares, each 6⅛" x 6⅛", for the B triangles
- 30 squares, each 3⅜" x 3⅜", for the E triangles

From the assorted scraps, cut:

- 144 squares, each 2½" x 2½", for the C triangles
- 36 squares, each 2⅞" x 2⅞", for the D triangles

From the light pastel print, cut:

- 5 strips, each 4½" x 42", for the side outer borders
- 4 strips, each 4½" x 30⅜", for the top and bottom outer borders (panels 1 and 3)
- 2 strips, each 4½" x 24⅞", for the top and bottom outer borders (panel 2)

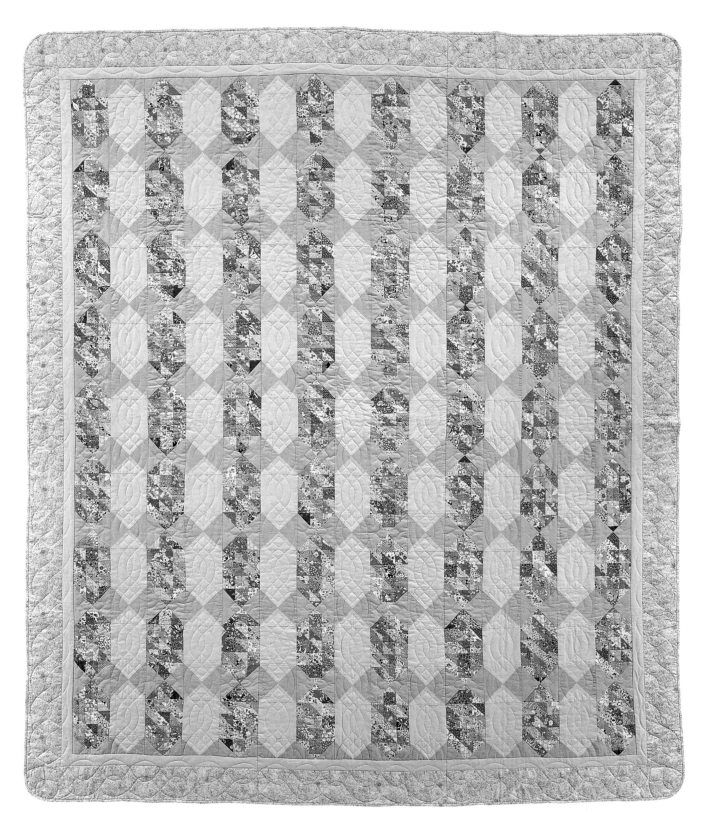

Pieced Pastel Pleasures, 84⅛" x 98¾", by Georgia J. Bonesteel.

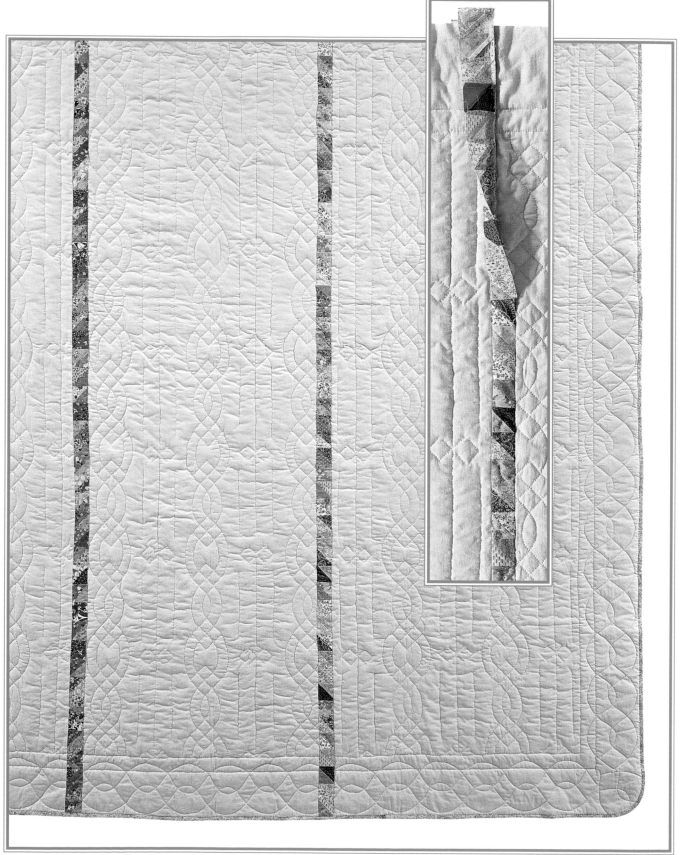

Quilt back and detail.

Assembling the Elongated Hexagons

1. Place two 5" x 7½" rectangles right sides together, aligning the raw edges. On the lighter fabric, draw a grid of six 2½" squares, marking the diagonals with a solid line.

    Mark a dashed line ¼" from each side of the diagonal lines. Stitch on the dashed lines, proceeding as indicated by the arrows in the illustration. Cut the grid into squares, then cut each square along its marked diagonal to make 2 half-square triangle units. Each grid will yield twelve 2⅛" half-square triangles. Repeat for each of the 76 rectangle pairs to make a total of 912 half-square triangle units. "Prune" all dog ears.

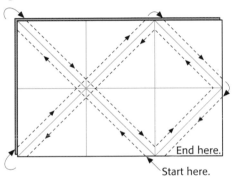

Start here.
End here.

2. Join 3 half-square triangle units to make a row, then join 3 rows to make a Nine Patch block as shown. Press the seams in alternating directions from row to row, so opposing seams nest, for easy, accurate piecing. Make 72 Nine Patch blocks. You'll have some half-square triangle units left over—we'll get to these soon!

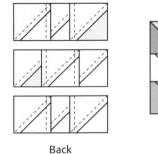

Back

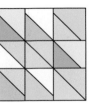

Front
Make 72.

3. Release seam allowances at intersections as shown. (You'll be opening the square-to-square seams to within a thread of the seam that joins the rows.) Opening the seam allowances lets you create a "twirl" and reduce bulk at these busy intersections.

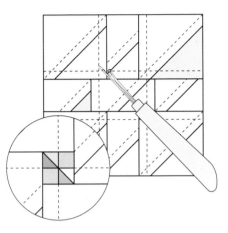

4. Cut each 2½" scrap square in half diagonally for a total of 288 half-square C triangles. Cut each 2⅞" scrap square twice diagonally for a total of 144 quarter-square D triangles.

5. Join a C triangle to opposite sides of a leftover half-square triangle unit. Refer to the illustration to be sure that you are sewing the triangles to the correct sides of the square! Top with a D triangle to create a large triangle unit as shown. Repeat to make 144 large triangle units.

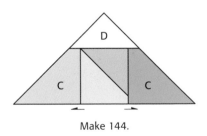

Make 144.

6. Sew 1 large triangle unit to the top and 1 to the bottom of a Nine Patch block. Refer to the diagram on page 32 to be sure you have positioned the block correctly. Repeat to make 72 elongated hexagons.

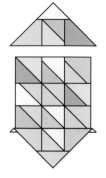

NOTE: *You'll still have leftover half-square triangle units. Set these aside. You'll use them later, on the back.*

7. Cut each 3⅜" lavender square once diagonally to make 60 half-square E triangles. Cut 32 of the 6⅛" lavender squares twice diagonally to make 128 quarter-square B triangles. Working on a design wall or other large flat surface, arrange 8 vertical rows of 9 hexagons each, inserting lavender B and E triangles to complete each row. Refer to the quilt diagram on page 33 for guidance. For now, leave space on each side of the hexagon rows. Pieced rows will be added later.

8. Stitch 2 lavender B triangles to all but the top and bottom hexagons in each row as shown.

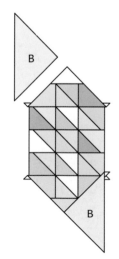

9. Sew the pointy hexagons into rows. Add the 2 B triangles (1 top, 1 bottom) and the 4 E triangles (2 top, 2 bottom) to complete each row.

Assembling the Alternate Pieced Rows

1. Use 28 of the 6⅛" blue squares and all the remaining 6⅛" lavender squares to quick-piece 28 quarter-square units: Place a blue and lavender square right sides together. Draw a solid diagonal cutting line on the top square. Mark a dashed line ¼" from each side of the cutting line, then stitch on the dashed lines. Cut along the solid line, prune the dog ears, then press the seams toward the lavender triangle.

    Place the 2 half-square triangles right sides together, blue to lavender, nesting the seams. Draw a second solid diagonal line as shown, and once again mark and stitch ¼" on each side of the diagonal. Cut the triangles apart and press, "pruning" the dog ears and trimming the quarter-square units to exactly 5⅜" x 5⅜". Make 56 quarter-square triangle units.

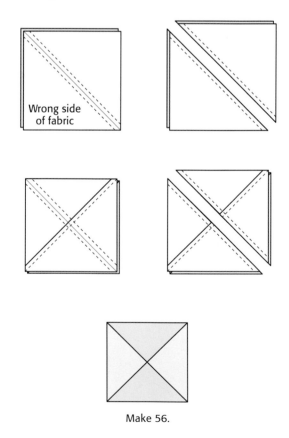

Wrong side of fabric

Make 56.

2. Join 8 quarter-square triangle units and 9 of the 5⅜" blue A squares to make an alternate pieced row. Refer to the quilt diagram at right as needed. Make 7 rows.

3. Cut each remaining 6⅛" blue square twice diagonally to yield quarter-square triangles. Add a remaining lavender E triangle to each short side of a blue B triangle as shown. Make 14 of these units, and add 1 to the top and 1 to the bottom of each alternate pieced row.

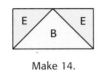

Make 14.

Assembling the Rows

THIS quilt is assembled in 3 vertical panels.

1. Referring to the diagram at right, piece 3 vertical panels, alternating hexagon and alternate pieced rows.

2. Stitch a side inner border to the left edge of panel 1 and to the right edge of panel 3. Add 2" x 24⅞" inner border strips to the top and bottom of panel 2, and 2" x 26⅜" inner border strips to the tops and bottoms of panels 1 and 3.

3. Using diagonal seams (see the tip box on page 24), join the 4½" x 42" outer border strips end to end to make 2 side outer borders, each 4½" x 91¼". Sew the side outer borders to panels 1 and 2, then add the appropriate top and bottom outer borders to the panels.

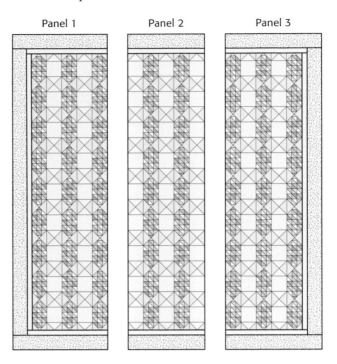

Panel 1   Panel 2   Panel 3

Quilting and Finishing

1. Cut batting and backing to the same size as the 3 panels, layer, and baste.

2. Hand or machine quilt as desired. The sample was quilted by hand in keeping with its traditional appearance. If desired, use a dinner plate or a flexicurve (page 11) to round the 4 outer corners as shown in the photo.

3. Piece the leftover half-square triangle units into 2 long strips of 60 units each. Join the quilted panels, using the row-to-row construction method (page 17). Use the pieced strips to finish the quilt back with accent binding (page 18).

4. Cut the 32" square of fabric into 2½"-wide strips for binding. There is enough fabric to cut strips on the straight of grain or on the bias, whichever you prefer. Bind the quilt to finish.

◆§ Tangram Teasers §◆

Gather your "groupies," call all your quilting friends, and announce a tangram challenge!

A tangram is a Chinese puzzle consisting of a square card or board cut into five triangles, a square, and a parallelogram. These shapes can then be recombined into a variety of configurations—the perfect puzzle for quilters.

Several years ago I proposed a tangram challenge to our Western North Carolina Quilters Guild in Hendersonville. According to our rules, the block was limited to solid colors (including black and white), each template could be used no more than twice, the parallelogram (diamond-shaped piece) could be reversed, and any finished-size square or rectangular block would be acceptable.

Years later I assembled the blocks into sections for lap quilting. You'll notice in the instructions that each section in a row is the same width, but the sections vary in length. (With a little planning—and the addition of a few spacer strips—it's possible to use unequal sections.) The instructions for "Tangram Teasers" call for a 12" block, but—since I show you how to draw your own—you can make the block any size.

Materials
(44"-WIDE FABRIC)

- 1 yd. *each* of red, yellow, green, blue, white, and black solids for Tangram blocks
- 2 yds. *total* of black-and-white geometric prints (polka dots, stripes, plaids) for spacers
- 2⅛ yds. multicolored print for sashing and borders
- 1½ yds. *each* of 4 different fabrics for backing
- Queen-size batting (90" x 108")
- 32" x 32" square of fabric for binding (or substitute a scrappy variety of 2½"-wide strips for a total length of 380")

Drawing the Tangram Block

1. Draw a 12" square on graph paper. Divide the square in half along 1 diagonal.

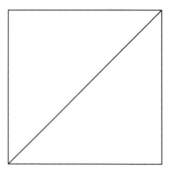

Tangram Teasers, 87" x 100¼", by Georgia J. Bonesteel and members of the Western North Carolina Quilters Guild: Jo Cadle, Janet Boland, Helen Shaver, Jane Shiley, Tim Cochran, Martine House, Bonnie Shaw, Mary Bowen, Polly Duncan, Esther Brown, Rita Wax, June Haynes, Trish Gabriel, Nana Nelson, Ruth Eaton, Gen Grundy, Pat Stirn, Mary Berry, Mary Pikoraitis, Linda Caudle, and Linda Sokalski.

Quilt back

2. Find and mark the midpoint on each short side of the upper left triangle. Connect the 2 midpoints.

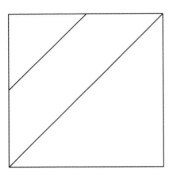

3. Find and mark the midpoint of the shorter diagonal line. Connect that midpoint with the opposite corner.

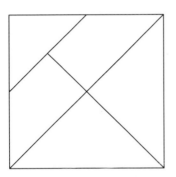

4. Find and mark the midpoint on the left-hand side of the bottom quarter-square triangle (a) and connect it to the corner of the small corner triangle (b) to make a square as shown.

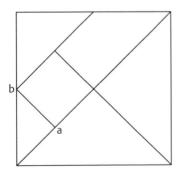

5. Find and mark the midpoint on the short right-hand side of the remaining quarter-square triangle (c) and connect it to the corner of the square (d) to make a par-allelogram and a small triangle. Label the shapes A through E as shown.

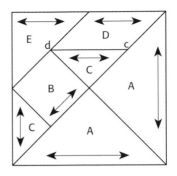

6. Transfer 1 of each shape to your favorite template material, adding ¼"-wide seam allowances to all sides. Label each template with the appropriate letter and mark grain-line arrows. Cut out the templates.

Cutting and Assembling the Sections

YOU'LL use the various solids and black-and-white geometric prints to cut pieces for the Tangram blocks and spacers. Vary the colors within each block and section for contrast, referring to the diagram on page 42 for guidance. All measurements include ¼"-wide seam allowances.

Section 1

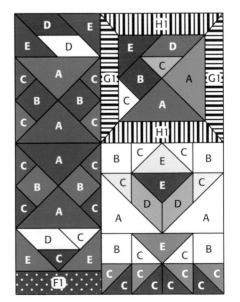

From the 6 solids and the various black-and-white geometric prints, cut:

- 8 A triangles, 9 B squares, 26 C triangles, 6 D pieces, and 8 E triangles
- 1 strip, 3¾" x 12½" (F1)*
- 2 strips, each 3" x 18½" (G1)*
- 2 strips, each 3½" x 17½" (H1)*

*You may need to adjust the length and/or width of the spacer strips after cutting so that the section fits together and finishes to the correct size.

Arrange the pieces as shown. Sew the pieces together, stitching the smaller shapes into larger square and rectangular units, then join the units. Because spacer strips H1 and G1 are cut to slightly different widths, they won't miter at an exact 45-degree angle. To achieve a smooth miter, stitch the strips to the Tangram block, lapping the extended ends of the H strips over the extended ends of the G strips. Fold back the end of 1 H strip on the diagonal, angling it so that its short edge aligns with the long edge of the G strip beneath it. Finger-press a crease, stitch, trim the seam allowance to ¼", then press the seam open. Repeat for all 4 corners.

Section 2

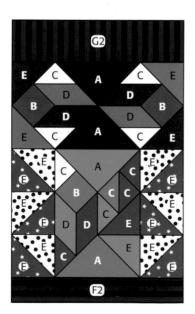

From the 6 solids and the various black-and-white geometric prints, cut:

- 4 A triangles, 3 B squares, 10 C triangles, 6 D pieces, and 18 E triangles
- 1 strip, 4" x 24½" (F2)
- 1 strip, 6¼" x 24½" (G2)

Arrange the pieces as shown. Sew the pieces together, stitching the smaller shapes into larger square and rectangle units, and then joining the units.

Section 3

From the 6 solids and the various black-and-white geometric prints, cut:

- 5 A triangles, 1 B square, 6 C triangles, 2 D pieces, and 1 E triangle
- 1 strip, 4½" x 16½" (F3)
- 5 squares, each 4½" x 4½" (G3)
- 1 strip, 4½" x 20" (H3)
- 1 strip, 3¾" x 13¼" (I3)
- 1 strip, 3¼" x 13¼" (J3)
- 1 strip, 4½" x 28" (K3)
- 1 strip, 4½" x 8¼" (L3)
- 1 strip, 4½" x 16½" (M3)
- 1 piece, 4¼" x 4½" (N3)

- 1 strip, 4¼" x 16½" (O3)
- 1 piece, 3¼" x 3¾" (P3)
- 1 strip, 4½" x 12½" (Q3)

Arrange the pieces as shown. Sew the pieces together, stitching the smaller shapes into larger square and rectangle units, and then joining the units.

Section 4

From the 6 solids and the various black-and-white geometric prints, cut:

- 6 A triangles, 4 B squares, 8 C triangles, 4 D pieces, and 4 E triangles
- 1 strip, 6½" x 12½" (F4)
- Randomly piece scraps together and then trim to make 1 strip, 5½" x 24½" (G4)

Arrange the pieces as shown. Sew the pieces together, stitching the smaller shapes into larger square and rectangle units, and then joining the units.

Section 5

From the 6 solids and the various black-and-white geometric prints, cut:

- 4 A triangles, 2 B squares, 4 C triangles, 2 D pieces, and 18 E triangles

Arrange the pieces as shown. Sew the pieces together, stitching the smaller shapes into larger square and rectangle units, and then joining the units.

Section 6

From the 6 solids and the various black-and-white geometric prints, cut:

- 4 A triangles, 2 B squares, 4 C triangles, 2 D pieces, and 2 E triangles
- 4 squares, each 12⅞" x 12⅞"; cut each square once diagonally to yield 4 triangles (F6) for spacers

Arrange the pieces as shown. Sew the pieces together, stitching the smaller shapes into larger square and rectangle units, and then joining the units.

Section 7

From the 6 solids and the various black-and-white geometric prints, cut:

- ♦ 2 A triangles, 4 B squares, 8 C triangles, 4 D pieces, and 4 E triangles
- ♦ 1 square, 10⅞" x 10⅞"; cut the square once diagonally to yield 2 triangles (F7) for spacers
- ♦ 1 square, 12⅞" x 12⅞"; cut the square once diagonally to yield 2 triangles (G7) for spacers
- ♦ 2 strips, each 1½" x 27½" (H7)
- ♦ 2 strips, each 4" x 23" (I7)

Arrange the pieces as shown. Set aside the I7 and 47 spacer strips and the F7 triangles. Sew the remaining pieces together, stitching the smaller shapes into larger square and rectangle units, and then joining the units. Sew the I7 spacers to the pieced unit, and then trim them even with the section's edges. Add the F7 triangles and the H7 strips to finish.

Section 8

From the 6 solids and the various black-and-white geometric prints, cut:

- ♦ 8 A triangles, 4 B squares, 8 C triangles, 4 D pieces, and 4 E triangles
- ♦ 2 strips, each 3½" x 12½" (F8)

Arrange the pieces as shown. Sew the pieces together, stitching the smaller shapes into larger square and rectangle units, and then joining the units.

Section 9

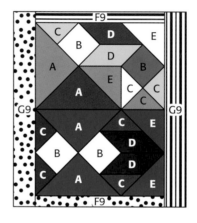

From the 6 solids and the various black-and-white geometric prints, cut:

- ♦ 4 A triangles, 4 B squares, 8 C triangles, 4 D pieces, and 4 E triangles
- ♦ 2 strips, each 2" x 18½" (F9)
- ♦ 2 strips, each 3½" x 27½" (G9)

Arrange the pieces as shown. Sew the pieces together, stitching the smaller shapes into larger square and rectangle units, and then joining the units.

Assembling the Quilt

CUT the following strips, then frame each section with the appropriate sashing strips and borders as shown.

From the multicolored print, cut:

- 2 strips, each 2½" x 39¾", for the sashing (sections 1, 2)
- 4 strips, each 2½" x 24½", for the sashing (sections 4, 5, 6)
- 2 strips, each 2½" x 26½", for the sashing (section 5)
- 2 strips, each 2½" x 31½", for the sashing (section 4)
- 2 strips, each 2½" x 27½", for the sashing (sections 7, 8)
- 2 strips, each 3½" x 34½", for the border (sections 1, 7)
- 2 strips, each 3½" x 26½", for the border (sections 2, 8)
- 4 strips, each 3½" x 27½", for the border (sections 3, 7, 9)
- 2 strips, each 3½" x 39¾", for the border (sections 1, 3)
- 2 strips, each 3½" x 28½", for the border (sections 4, 6)

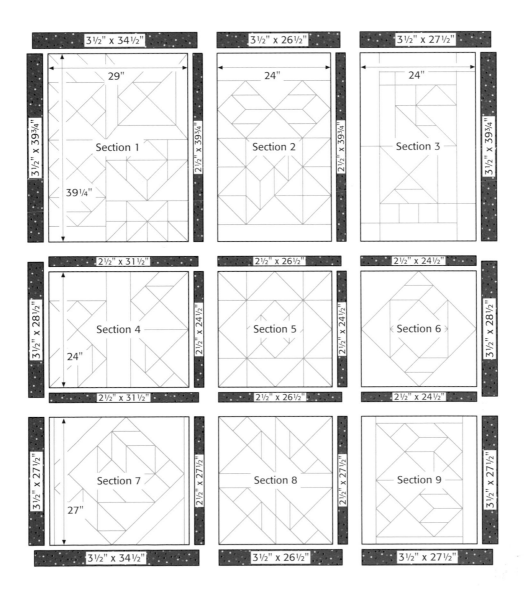

Preparing the Sections for Quilting

1. Cut a panel of batting the same size as each section.

2. Cut the various backing fabrics crosswise into 42"-long strips ranging from 9" to 10" wide. Piece these strips to make backing panels the same size as each section. Note how I changed the direction of the strips in each panel to create a "two for one," reversible quilt.

Pieced back

3. Layer each section with the appropriate batting and backing panel, and baste.

Quilting and Finishing

1. Quilt the sections and sashing strips as desired. For the sample quilt, a swirl-patterned stencil was designed to fit the various squares, rectangles, and triangles.

Leave a ½" unquilted margin along all connecting edges on the inside sections. Wait until the sections are joined to quilt the borders.

> ❧ *Experiment to create your own quilting designs for this quilt. Cut "instant" quilting templates from heavy manila folders or Con-Tact paper.*

2. Join the sections using the block-to-block (in this case, section-to-section) connection (page 16). In the sample, sections were joined by machine from the back and finished by hand on the front. Wavy-line machine quilting finished the borders.

3. Cut the 32" square of binding fabric into 2½"-wide binding strips. There is enough fabric to cut strips on the straight of grain or on the bias, whichever you prefer. Bind the quilt to finish.

Home Sweet Home Sampler

I gravitate toward samplers. In the quilt world, they remain a mainstay of classes taught as stepping-stones to more advanced work. The variety of block designs and construction methods provide splendid learning opportunities, and the more we are challenged, the greater the array of settings and color arrangements we seem to devise. But perhaps you haven't yet seen a sampler designed as a house!

"Home Sweet Home Sampler" developed from a quilt challenge among my Freedom Escape Quilt "groupies." Each member chose a color scheme and all the other members contributed a block in that color scheme. The contributor chose the block design and the size. In the end, each quilter had a collection of different blocks in her preferred colors.

I chose off-white for my color scheme, and I received twenty-two wonderfully different, odd-sized blocks. I framed some of them as a door, two as windows, then added a triangular roofline, complete with chimney. A tree with dimensional leaves provided the finishing touch.

Here are guidelines for creating successful samplers:

- *Consider the final size. Do you want your quilt to be a bedcover or wall hanging? Prepare the backing fabric and hang it on your design wall to mark the quilt's outermost boundaries.*

- *Consider spacer fabrics. Unless your quilt will be arranged block to block, you'll need setting fabric between the blocks, rows, or sections. Experiment until you find an appropriate choice—or choices.*

- *Square up all blocks, which includes pruning the dog ears (page 6). Label each block with its finished measurements. You may find it convenient to draw and cut up a reduced diagram on graph paper, so you can rearrange the pieces on a grid.*

- *Study your arrangement for a while so as not to rush into the final setting decision, and ask your family and quilting companions for suggestions.*

- *Once the setting is determined, map out the spacer sizes between blocks, rows, and sections, allowing for ¼" seam allowances on all sides. Add borders and/or sashing to complete and frame the final design.*

- *When joining blocks and sections that vary in size, plan to assemble the entire quilt before quilting it.*

Home Sweet Home Sampler, 62" x 78", by Georgia J. Bonesteel and members of Freedom Escape Quilt.

❧ Indian Trails ❧

Penny Wortman has had a quilt in every book I've written. As a student of mine years ago, she learned her lessons well and moved on to make outstanding quilts via the "quilt as you go" method. Penny re-creates the past in her quilts by choosing classic patterns and vintage fabrics. Her fine workmanship always shines through in the finished product.

Finished Block Size: 15"

Materials
(44"-wide fabric)

- 2⅛ yds. white-on-white print for blocks and borders
- ⅜ yd. dark pink print for blocks
- 12 different 12" x 16" green prints for blocks
- ¼ yd. medium pink print for corner squares
- 1 yd. medium green print for sashing
- ¼ yd. dark green print for border corner squares
- A *wide* assortment of dark and light scraps to total approximately 5 yds. for blocks and borders
- Twin-size batting (72" x 90")
- 4⅝ yds. fabric for backing
- 28" x 28" square of fabric for binding

Cutting

MAKE templates for pieces A through G by transferring the patterns on pages 50–51 to your preferred template material. Label each template with the appropriate letter and grain-line arrow. All templates and cutting measurements include ¼"-wide seam allowances.

From the white-on-white print, cut:
- 48 B pieces for blocks
- 244 D pieces for borders
- 4 E regular and 4 E reverse pieces for border corner squares

- 8 G regular and 8 G reverse pieces for borders

From the dark pink print, cut:
- 12 squares, each 4⅞" x 4⅞", for the blocks

From *each* of the 12" x 16" green prints, cut:
- 4 A pieces (48 total) for the blocks

From the medium pink print, cut:
- 20 squares, each 2½" x 2½", for the corner squares

From the medium green print, cut:
- 31 strips, each 2½" x 15½", for the sashing

From the dark green print, cut:
- 4 F pieces for the border corner squares

From the assortment of scrap fabrics, cut:
- 126 C pieces for the borders

Assembling the Paper-Pieced Arcs

1. Make 48 copies of the "Indian Trails" paper-piecing foundation on the pullout.

2. Turn a paper foundation so the wrong side faces you. Pin a dark scrap, right side up, over the middle triangle in the arc. Be sure the scrap is big enough to leave a ¼" seam allowance. Position a light scrap on top of

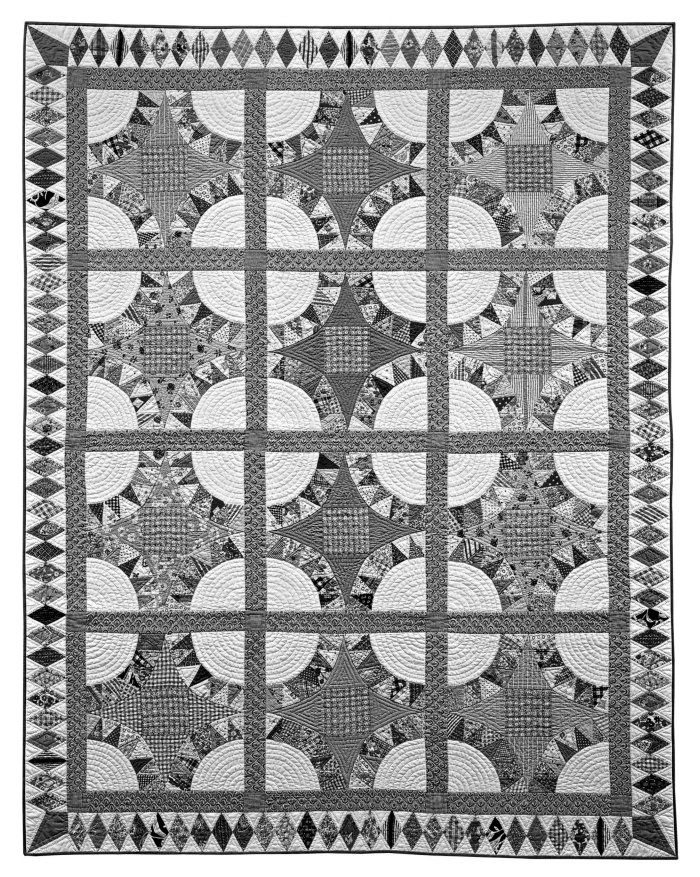

Indian Trails, 61" x 78", by Penelope Wortman.

the dark scrap, right sides together, making sure the second piece is big enough to generously cover the adjacent triangle. Holding the scraps in place, turn the paper to the front. Using a smaller-than-usual stitch (18 to 20 stitches per inch), sew along 1 side of the triangle directly on the marked line. (The smaller stitches will make it easier to remove the paper later.) Trim the seam allowance to ¼" and press the seam open.

Continue adding scraps, working out from the center of the arc, alternating dark and light fabrics. Remember to trim seam allowances before pressing them open.

3. When the arc is complete, trim any excess fabric from the outer edges. Fold the paper-pieced arc and a B quarter circle in half to find and mark their midpoints. Place the arc and the B piece right sides together, pin carefully to match ends and midpoints, then stitch. Make 48 of these quarter-circle units, and label them Unit 1.

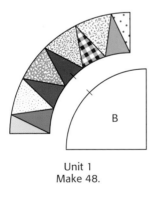

Unit 1
Make 48.

> ⧉ *You'll find it easier to stitch the curved edges if you match and pin the midpoints and the ends of pieces A and B with the pieced arc. Fabric has more give than paper at the sewing machine. Sew with the pieced arc down, against the feed dogs.*

Assembling the Block

1. Sew 4 matching A pieces to each 4⅞" dark pink square as shown. Make 12 and label them Unit 2.

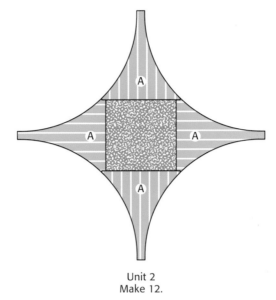

Unit 2
Make 12.

2. Pinning carefully to match ends and midpoints, stitch a curved Unit 1 to each curved edge of a Unit 2 to complete the block. Make 12 blocks. Remove the paper foundations.

Make 12.

Assembling the Quilt

> ❧ *Penny chose to quilt Indian Trails in 3 horizontal sections, including the pieced outside borders. The backing was cut straight, and the angled diamonds stitched after quilting was completed.*
>
> *To simplify the instructions, I am suggesting you assemble the entire quilt top before lap-quilting.*

ARRANGE the blocks, sashing strips, and medium pink corner squares as shown. Sew together the sashing strips and corner squares between rows, then sew together the rows of sashing strips and blocks. Join the rows, pinning carefully to match the seams.

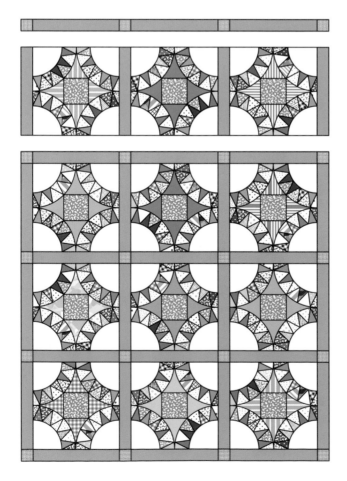

Piecing and Attaching the Borders

1. Placing right sides together, sew white-on-white D triangles to opposite sides of a scrap C diamond as shown. Make 118 triangle-diamond units.

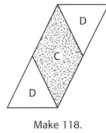

Make 118.

2. Join 34 triangle-diamond units to make each side border. In a similar fashion, join 25 triangle-diamond units to make the top and then the bottom border.

3. Stitch G triangles to the left edges of a remaining C diamond as shown. Add a D triangle to the upper right edge to complete the unit. Make 4 and label them Unit 3.

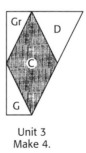

Unit 3
Make 4.

4. Stitch G triangles to the right edges of the remaining C diamonds as shown. Add a D triangle to the lower left edge to complete the unit. Make 4 and label them Unit 4.

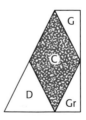

Unit 4
Make 4.

5. Complete each pieced border by adding a Unit 3 to its left edge and a Unit 4 to its right edge as shown.

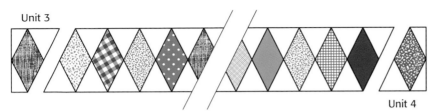

Unit 3

Unit 4

6. Join white regular and reverse E triangles to the long edges of an F piece as shown. Make 4 of these corner squares.

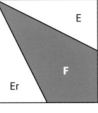

Border Corner Square
Make 4.

7. Pin a side border to the left and right edges of the quilt, carefully matching ends and midpoints. Attach the side borders.

8. Sew a border corner square to each end of both the top and bottom borders. Attach these borders to the quilt.

❧ Call upon the "fudge factor" if you need to adjust the borders to fit. If necessary, take a slightly fuller—or skimpier—seam every now and then, and check your pro-gress as you go.

Quilting and Finishing

1. Divide the backing fabric into 2 panels of equal length (83¼"), remove the selvages, and join along the selvage edges to make a single large backing. Center the quilt top and the batting over the backing, and baste.

2. Quilt as desired.

3. Cut the 28" square of fabric into 2½"-wide strips for binding. There is enough fabric to cut strips on the straight of grain or bias, whichever you prefer. Bind the quilt to finish.

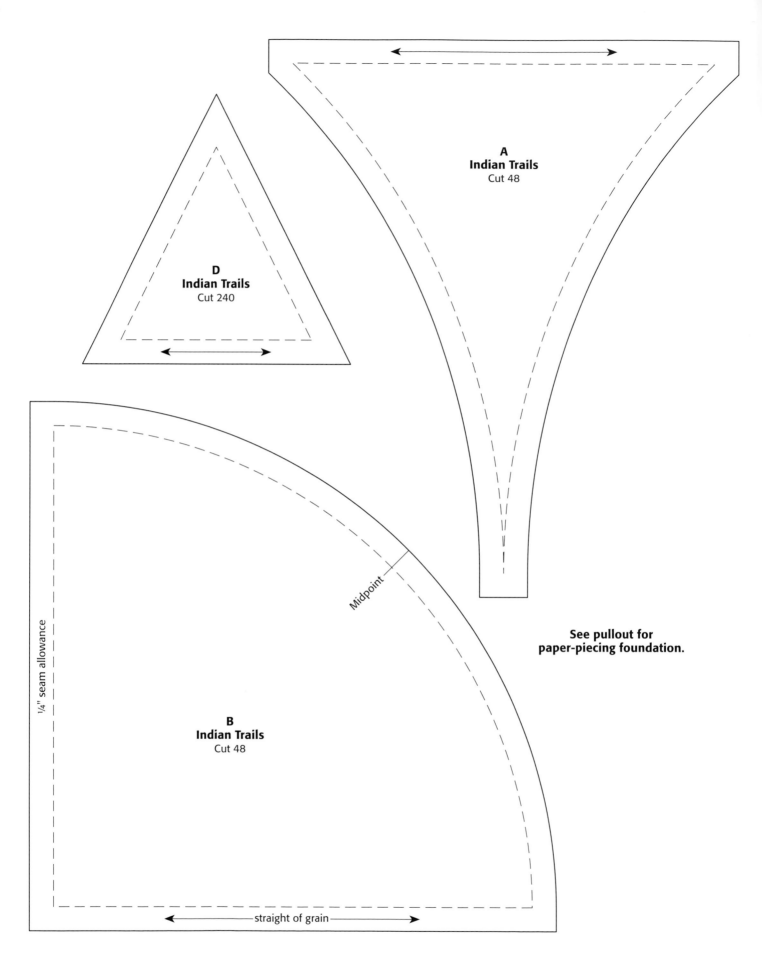

A
Indian Trails
Cut 48

D
Indian Trails
Cut 240

See pullout for
paper-piecing foundation.

Midpoint

¼" seam allowance

B
Indian Trails
Cut 48

straight of grain

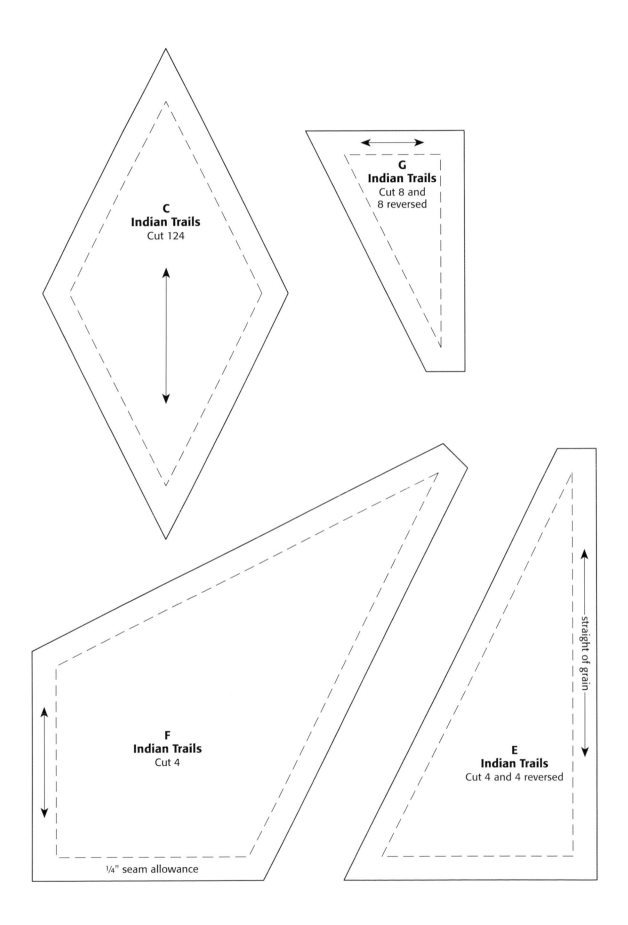

C
Indian Trails
Cut 124

G
Indian Trails
Cut 8 and
8 reversed

F
Indian Trails
Cut 4

¼" seam allowance

E
Indian Trails
Cut 4 and 4 reversed

straight of grain

I've Got the Blues

᠍

Blue seems to be a favorite color of quilters everywhere,
so why not use some of those beautiful blue fabrics you've been
collecting and make a quilt? The fabrics used in this section
are varied—from casual denim to elegant toile—so you're sure to
find a pattern that fits your stash and your mood.

Tree of Life

A preprinted fabric panel finds life as a quilt, with oversized quarter-square triangle units accenting three sides. I acquired the panel on a trip to Den Haan & Wagenmakers in Amsterdam. Several years passed before a just-right bedroom decor, featuring a king-size four-poster bed, inspired the completion of "Tree of Life." The quilt includes a medley of prints that pick up the many shades of blue in the center panel.

Do you have a "cheater" block or a special printed panel waiting for new life in a quilt? Figuring proper measurements on paper is the key to success for any quilt, and for this one, your particular panel and desired bed size will help determine the width and length of the patchwork borders. In addition to adjusting the number of pieced border squares to accommodate both the center panel and the bed, you can also adjust the size of the blocks. Be sure to include enough for a pillow tuck and for sufficient drop on the sides.

Materials

(44"-WIDE FABRIC)

♦ A large printed panel (in this case, 68½" x 90½")

♦ 6 yds. *total* of assorted blue scraps for pieced borders

♦ ⅝ yd. white-on-white muslin for middle border

♦ 10½ yds. fabric for backing

♦ Batting, approximately 126" x 122" (piece if necessary)

♦ 36" x 36" square of fabric for binding

Cutting

All measurements include ¼"-wide seam allowances.

From the assorted blue scraps, cut:

♦ 33 squares, each 13¼" x 13¼", for the pieced borders

♦ 4 squares, each 6⅞" x 6⅞", for the pieced borders

From the white-on-white muslin, cut:

♦ 8 strips, each 2½" x 42", for the middle side and bottom borders

Assembling the Pieced Borders

1. Sort 32 of the 13¼" blue squares into 16 contrasting pairs, right sides together. Draw a solid diagonal cutting line on each top square. Mark a dashed line ¼" from each side of the cutting line, then stitch on the dashed lines. Cut the triangles apart on

Tree of Life, 120" x 116", by Georgia J. Bonesteel, quilted by Shirley Henion.

the solid line, "prune" the dog ears, then press the seams toward the darker triangle.

Place 2 half-square triangles right sides together, nesting the seams. Draw a second solid diagonal line as shown, and once again mark and stitch ¼" on each side of the diagonal. Cut the triangles apart and press, trimming the quarter-square units to exactly 12" x 12". Make 32 quarter-square triangle units. Stack and label these Block 1.

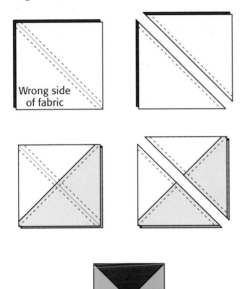

Block 1
12" x 12"
Make 32.

2. Draw a 10" x 12" and a 9" x 12" rectangle on graph paper. Divide each rectangle from corner to corner along both diagonals, and label the triangles as shown. Trace the C through F triangles onto template material, adding ¼"-wide seam allowances to all sides and marking the template letters and grain-line arrows. Cut out the templates.

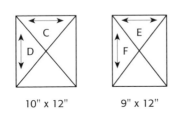

10" x 12"   9" x 12"

3. From the remaining assorted blue fabrics, cut 8 C triangles, 8 D triangles, 16 E triangles, and 16 F triangles. Use the C and D triangles to piece 4 of Block 2. Use the E and F triangles to piece 8 of Block 3.

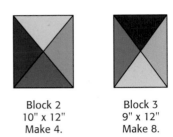

Block 2   Block 3
10" x 12"   9" x 12"
Make 4.   Make 8.

4. Cut the remaining 13¼" blue square twice diagonally to yield 4 quarter-square A triangles. Cut the four 6⅞" squares in half diagonally to yield 8 half-square B triangles. Sew B triangles to the short sides of each A triangle to make 4 half-block units as shown.

Half-block unit
Make 4.

5. Join and cut the 2½" x 42" border strips as needed to make two 2½" x 104½" side borders and one 2½" x 92½" bottom border. Sew the joining seams diagonally (see the tip box on page 24).

6. Arrange the pieced blocks and muslin strips around 3 edges of the center panel. Each side edge includes double rows of pieced border blocks separated by a muslin strip. The inner border is made from 8 of Block 1, the outer border from 7 of Block 1. A half-block unit begins each of the pieced rows.

The bottom edge includes an inner and outer row composed of one Block 1, two Block 2, and four Block 3, separated by the bottom muslin border strip.

7. Piece the blocks to form the inner and outer border strips. Attach the borders in the following order: inner pieced bottom border, inner pieced side borders, bottom muslin strip, and then side muslin strips. Align the upper edges of the remaining side borders with the upper edge of the quilt, and attach those next. Align the mid-point of the bottom edge of the quilt with the midpoint of the outer bottom border, and attach.

Quilting and Finishing

1. Fold the length of backing fabric into thirds and cut it into 3 panels, each 42" x 126". Remove the selvages, and join the panels as shown.

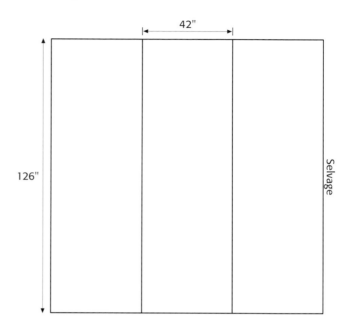

2. Center the batting and quilt top over the pieced backing, and baste.

3. Quilt as desired.

4. Cut the 36" square of fabric into 2½"-wide bias strips for binding. Bind the quilt to finish.

❧ Toile-aholic ❧

Toile fabric has always captured my heart. It speaks of another, more formal time, yet when mixed with solids and woven checks it takes on a country flair. You can use any large print—not just toile—and still achieve a decorator look, so start your search now and collect a multitude of toile or other large-scale prints.

Materials
(44"-WIDE FABRIC)

- ⅔ yd. *each* of 12 different toile or large-scale, non-directional prints for A, D, G, and J pieces*
- ⅔ yd. *each* of 12 woven checks/plaids to coordinate with the toile fabrics for B and H strips
- 1 yd. *each* of coordinating light and dark solids for C sashes, E and F triangles, and I pieces
- 7½ yds. fabric for backing**
- Batting, approximately 91" x 127" (piece if necessary)
- 35" x 35" square of fabric for binding

*Or substitute 7 yds. total of a single fabric.
**Some creative piecing here might save fabric. For example, try adding a border around leftover toile for a pieced backing.

Making Templates

BEFORE you cut, you'll need to make templates for some of the pattern pieces. Make templates for B, C, G, H, I, and J by tracing the patterns on the pullout.

You'll need to draw your own patterns for the A and D triangles. To make the A template, draw a straight 24¼" line on ¼" graph paper. Using a ruler that shows a 45-degree angle,

identify the 45-degree angle at each end of the drawn line and draw two 17⅛" lines to complete the triangle as shown. Label this triangle A.

To make the D template, draw a 90-degree angle with 12⅜" "legs." Connect the free ends with a 17½" diagonal line as shown. Label this triangle D.

Transfer the triangles to template material. (You don't need to add seam allowances; they are already included.) Label the templates, add arrows to indicate grain line, and cut out the templates.

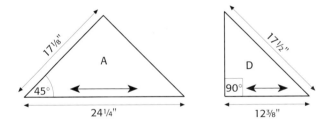

Cutting

MOST toile is directional, so be sure to watch the direction of the fabric when positioning the A and D templates. All measurements include ¼"-wide seam allowances.

For quick and easy regular and reverse pieces—such as for piece G in this pattern—fold the fabric right sides together, trace the template, and cut. You'll get perfect mirror-image pieces.

Toile-aholic, 85½" x 121½", by Georgia J. Bonesteel.

From the toile fabrics, cut:

- 9 different pairs of matching mirror-image A triangles (18 total)
- 3 different sets of 4 matching mirror-image D triangles (12 total)
- 70 regular and 70 reverse G pieces (140 total)
- 4 different pairs of matching J triangles, 1 regular and 1 reverse per pair (8 total)

From the check/plaid fabrics, cut:

- 4 B strips to coordinate with each toile fabric (48 total)

From the light solid, cut:

- 24 C pieces for pieced sashing
- 5 squares, each 5⅛" x 5⅛", for piece E
- 5 squares, each 3⅞" x 3⅞", for piece F
- 2 I pieces for corner squares

From the dark solid, cut:

- 24 C pieces for pieced sashing
- 5 squares, each 5⅛" x 5⅛", for piece E
- 5 squares, each 3⅞" x 3⅞", for piece F
- 2 I pieces for corner squares

Assembling the Quilt Top

1. Stitch light and dark C pieces together in pairs as shown to make 24 sashing units.

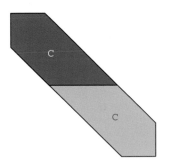

2. Stitch a matching pair of B strips to the 2 short sides of 2 matching A triangles, stopping and backstitching ¼" from the corner where they meet. (Stopping at the corner will allow you to miter later.)

3. Lay out the quilt top (minus the borders) in 6 horizontal rows as shown. Laying out the top before you stitch allows you to arrange the matching D triangles and B strips so that they carry over from row to row. Remember to alternate the position of the dark and light ends of the pieced C sashes, and watch the direction of the toile fabrics.

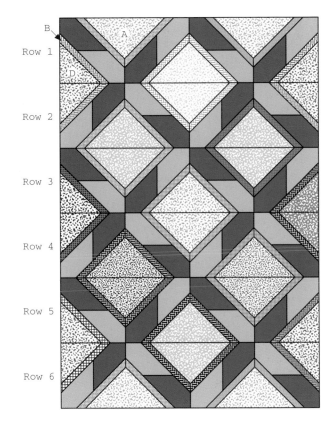

4. Sew the long sides of the pieced C sashes to the A /B units, and complete the mitered seams as shown.

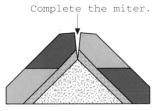

Complete the miter.

5. Sew the remaining B strips to the long edges of the D triangles. Complete each row by attaching the B/D unit to the pieced C sash. Don't join the rows yet.

Assembling and Attaching the Borders

1. If you look at the photo on page 58, you'll notice that the B strips framing the outer A and D triangles extend into the borders. From the remaining check/plaid fabric, trace and cut 10 pairs of H strips, for a total of 20 strips. Cut each pair from the same fabric as the B strips they will be extending.

2. You will need to construct 2 different pieced border units. These units will be joined in mirror-image pairs. In preparation, cut each 3⅜" light and dark F square in half diagonally for a total of 20 half-square triangles. Repeat for each 5⅜" E square.

3. For Border Unit 1, join 7 assorted G pieces along their long sides, aligning the short top and bottom edges. Add a light F triangle to the right bottom edge of the pieced unit, and stitch in place as shown. Trim the right edge of the unit even with the straight edge of the triangle.

    Add the H strip by matching its longest edge with the left edge of the pieced unit. Finish the unit by adding a light E triangle

to the upper left corner as shown. Make 4 of Border Unit 1 for the top and bottom borders, then repeat to make another 6, this time using dark E and F triangles, for the side borders.

4. For Border Unit 2, join 7 assorted reverse G pieces, aligning the short top and bottom edges. Add a light F triangle to the lower left corner and stitch. Trim the left edge of the unit even with the straight edge of the triangle as shown. Add an H strip and a light E triangle to the right edge of the unit. Make 6 of Border Unit 2 for the side borders. Repeat to make another 4 for the top and bottom borders, substituting dark E and F triangles.

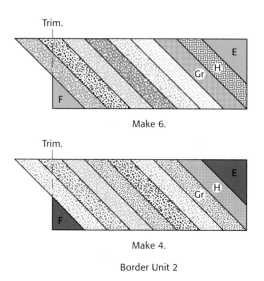

Border Unit 2

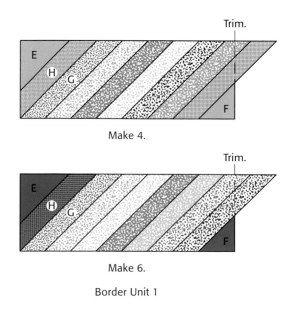

Border Unit 1

> 🐚 *Here's a tip to help you sew the proper H "extender" strip to the correct border unit. Lay out the rows of blocks as they will appear in the finished quilt, then piece the border units one at a time. Start in the lower left corner with the unit that begins the bottom border (Border Unit 1), and work your way counterclockwise around the quilt. As you complete each border unit, place it in position next to the quilt top.*

5. Attach the appropriate end border unit to each horizontal row, then join the rows, carefully matching the seams.

6. Sew matching J regular and reverse pieces to each I piece as shown to make the 4 corner squares.

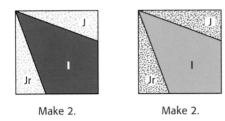

Make 2.   Make 2.

7. Join the appropriate 4 border units to make the top border. Add the corresponding dark or light I corner square to finish, then sew the border to the quilt. Repeat to make and add the bottom border.

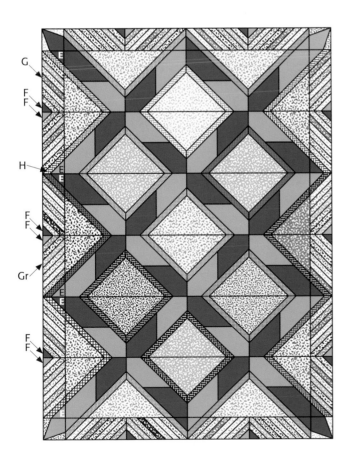

Since this quilt assembles in horizontal rows, it would also adapt to row-to-row lap quilting. If that is your preference, don't join the rows before basting and quilting. Refer instead to "Row to Row" on page 17 for instructions on how to assemble your quilt in sections.

Quilting and Finishing

1. Fold the length of backing fabric into thirds and cut it into 3 panels, each 42" x 90". Remove the selvages and join the panels as shown to make a large pieced backing.

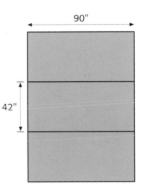

2. Position the backing so that the seams run horizontally, center the quilt top and batting over the backing, and baste.

3. Quilt as desired. My good intention of hand quilting failed due to the weight of the toile, but my sewing machine enabled me to quilt in an overall meandering motif. Depending on the fabrics you've chosen, you can quilt by hand or with your sewing machine, as you prefer.

4. Cut the 35" square of binding fabric into 2½"-wide strips. There is enough fabric to cut strips on the straight of grain or on the bias, whichever you prefer. Bind the quilt to finish.

So Dear to My Heart

Nothing is more crisp, clean, and inviting than a navy-and-white quilt. A smaller rendition of "Heart to Heart" (page 20), this lively interpretation is framed with a delightful parade of red and pink prairie-point hearts.

Materials

(44"-WIDE FABRIC)

- ¼ yd. *each* of 16 different navy prints for appliqués
- ⅝ yd. *total* of assorted navy prints for blocks*
- 1 yd. white-on-white print for appliqué backgrounds
- ½ yd. *total* of assorted red and pink scraps for squares and prairie points
- 1½ yds. fabric for backing
- Crib-size batting (45" x 60")

*Leftover appliqué fabrics can be included in the ⅝ yard total.

Cutting for Hearts

MAKE a template from the appropriate heart pattern on the pullout. Fold each of the sixteen ¼-yard navy prints in half right side out, and trace the template on the fold twice, as shown. Cut 2 hearts from each fabric, adding ¼" seam allowances to the fabric shapes as you cut, for a total of 32 hearts.

> ❧ *Making the heart template from freezer paper or Grid-Grip (page 110) allows you to iron the template directly onto fabric. You can cut the heart appliqués without having to trace them, and you can peel off and reuse the same template over and over again.*

Cutting for Blocks

From the navy prints for blocks, cut:
- 116 squares, each 2½" x 2½"

From the white-on-white, cut:
- 8 rectangles, each 8½" x 12½", for the backgrounds
- 16 rectangles, each 2½" x 8½", for the backgrounds

From the red and pink scraps, cut:
- 66 squares, each 2½" x 2½", for the blocks, Unit A, and prairie points
- 11 squares, each 4" x 4", for Unit A and corner units

So Dear to My Heart, 34" x 51" (plus prairie points), by Georgia J. Bonesteel.

Assembling the Background Blocks

1. Sew a 2½" navy square to each short end of a 2½" x 8½" rectangle. Make 10 units.

2. Sew a 2½" red or pink square to each short end of a 2½" x 8½" rectangle. Make 4 units.

3. Sew a 2½" red square and a 2½" blue square to opposite ends of the remaining two 2½" x 8½" rectangles.

4. Sew the pieced units to 8½" x 12½" rectangles as shown to make background blocks.

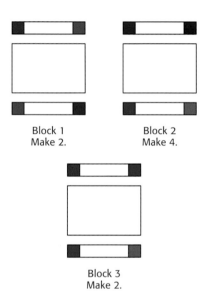

Block 1
Make 2.

Block 2
Make 4.

Block 3
Make 2.

Appliquéing the Blocks

LIGHTLY press each of the background blocks on both diagonals. Use these diagonal creases to position 2 matching pairs of navy hearts (points toward the center) on the background block as shown. Use your preferred method to appliqué the hearts in place.

ప్ *Here's the method I used to appliqué the hearts to the background blocks: Press a freezer paper or Grid-Grip template (without seam allowances) to the right side of a fabric heart. Straight-stitch just outside the paper edge to secure the heart to the block, then use appliqué scissors to trim the seam allowance right up to the paper. Remove the paper template and use a satin stitch to cover the raw edges and previous stitches. Placing a stabilizer underneath, against the feed dogs, ensures stable stitches.*

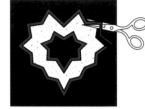

Stitch around template.   Trim.

Satin-stitch edges.

Assembling the Quilt Top

1. Cut each 4" red or pink square twice diagonally for a total of 44 quarter-square triangles. To make a corner unit, stitch four 2½" navy squares in a row, then add a red or pink triangle to each end as shown. Make 4 corner units.

Make 4.

2. Use 22 of the 2½" red and pink squares, all of the remaining red and pink triangles, and 2½" navy squares to make 6 pieced setting triangles as shown. Label these Unit A.

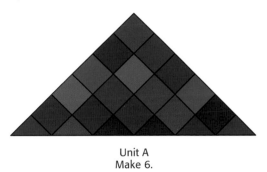

Unit A
Make 6.

3. Lay out the entire quilt top as shown. Be sure the appliqué blocks are positioned correctly. Join the blocks and setting triangles to make 4 diagonal rows, then sew the rows together. Add the corner units last.

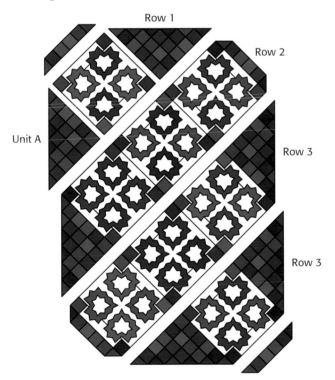

Row 1
Row 2
Row 3
Row 3
Unit A

4. Fold the remaining 2½" red and pink squares into prairie points as shown.

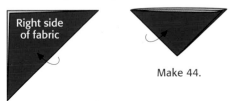

Right side
of fabric

Make 44.

5. Place the prairie points on the quilt top, overlapping corners as shown and aligning raw edges. The folded points should face the center of the quilt. Position the prairie points so that they will form red-and-pink hearts when they are stitched and flipped. Machine baste a scant ¼" from the raw edges to secure.

Prairie
points

Quilt
top

Finishing and Quilting

1. Cut the batting and backing to the same size as the quilt top. Layer the quilt components in the following order: batting; backing, right side up; then the quilt top, right side down. Pin to secure the layers. With the batting against the feed dogs, machine stitch ¼" from the raw edges all around the quilt sandwich. Leave an opening of approximately 6". Trim the seam as needed, then turn the quilt right side out and close the opening with invisible hand stitching.

2. Quilt as desired. In the sample quilt, the hearts were outlined with machine quilting (with the aid of a walking foot). Additional hand-quilted hearts were added to the background inside each appliquéd heart, and straight lines were quilted amid the pieced squares and triangles.

⇜ Hand in Heart Pillow ⇝

A third version of the classic heart shape explodes atop this large, colorful pillow done up in wool and secured with blanket-stitch embroidery. This no-quilting, patchwork-only project makes a welcome accent for any room.

Hand in Heart Pillow, 32" x 24", by Georgia J. Bonesteel

Materials

(44"-WIDE FABRIC)

- ½ yd. *each* of 2 different burgundy prints for corner triangles and borders
- 1 yd. complementary print or solid for backing and facings
- 1 contrasting, variegated wool or cotton print square, 20" x 20", for the heart
- 1 navy print square, 17½" x 17½", for the appliqué background
- ½ yd. *total* of assorted bright wool scraps for hand, circle, and star appliqués
- Skein of black embroidery thread
- 24" x 24" square pillow form
- 20" length of Velcro

Cutting

All measurements include ¼"-wide seam allowances.

From *each* of the burgundy prints, cut:

- 1 square, 13¼" x 13¼", for the corner triangles
- 2 rectangles, each 4½" x 12½", for the borders

From the backing fabric, cut:

- 1 rectangle, 24½" x 41", for the pillow back
- 2 rectangles, each 4½" x 24½", for the facings

Assembling the Pillow Top

1. Make heart, circle, and star templates from the "Hand in Heart" patterns on the pullout.

2. Trace the heart templates onto the 20" wool square. Cut out the pieces.

3. Carefully fold the navy print background square in half along both diagonals, finger-pressing to lightly crease. Center the heart on the background block, aligning the heart's center with the crease lines. Using black embroidery thread, hand stitch the heart to the block with an irregular (sometimes long, sometimes short) buttonhole stitch.

4. Trace the outline of your hand onto a wool scrap. Cut out the hand shape and secure it inside the heart, using an irregular buttonhole stitch.

5. Cut both burgundy squares in half diagonally to make a total of 4 half-square triangles. Position a set of same-fabric triangles on opposite sides of the heart block. Sew, then repeat to add the remaining triangles.

6. Using the templates made in step 1, trace 27 circles onto the assorted wool scraps. Referring to the photo on page 66, position the circles on the corner triangles, and secure them with an irregular buttonhole stitch. Trace the star template onto a wool scrap, then cut out the star. Center it above the heart, and buttonhole-stitch it in place.

7. Join 2 contrasting border rectangles along their short sides to make 2 border strips. Sew the borders to the 2 side edges of the pillow top, matching the border seams to the block points and placing contrasting burgundy prints adjacent to each other.

Finishing the Pillow

1. Place the facing strips and borders right sides together, aligning the edges. Stitch along the long edges, then turn the strips to the inside.

2. Fold a 4½" flap on each short side of the backing panel, wrong sides together. Press the flaps, then place the pillow top and backing right sides together, aligning the raw edges. Machine stitch along the top and the bottom edges, then turn the pillowcase right side out. To finish the top and bottom edges, hand sew a running stitch ¼" from each edge

3. Machine stitch along the border seam on 1 side of the pillowcase. Stitch Velcro inside the opposite edge along the border seam and flap edge. Insert the pillow form and secure the Velcro to complete.

❧ X Marks the Spot ❧

An inlaid wooden floor provided inspiration for this diagonal design with a Southwestern flair. Two shades of blue denim frame and accent the crisscross blocks. Gen Grundy, a faithful quilting friend, translated the design from paper to fabric.

Finished Block size: 18"

Materials

(44"-WIDE FABRIC)

- 8 yds. Southwestern print for blocks, outer border, and backing
- 1 yd. brick red solid for blocks
- ¾ yd. medium brown solid for blocks
- ⅛ yd. *each* of 6 solids, ranging from beige through peach to terra cotta, for blocks
- ½ yd. mottled turquoise print for blocks
- ¼ yd. yellow solid for stars
- 1¼ yds. light blue denim for piece I (inner sashing)*
- 2⅛ yds. dark blue denim for piece H (outer sashing), inner borders, and binding*
- Full-size batting (81" x 96")

*Or substitute "denim-look" cotton.

Cutting

All measurements include ¼"-wide seam allowances.

NOTE: *Before cutting, you need to make templates for pieces A–F, H, and I. Trace the patterns on the pullout onto template material, and transfer the template letters and grain-line arrows to the templates.*

From the Southwestern print, cut:

- 2 panels, each 42" x 90", for the backing
- 2 strips, each 6" x 67½", for the top and bottom outer borders

- 2 strips, each 6" x 85½", for the side outer borders
- 12 piece B for blocks

From the brick red solid, cut:

- 24 piece A for blocks

From the medium brown solid, cut:

- 24 regular and 24 reverse F pieces for blocks

From *each* of the 5 darkest beige to terra cotta solids, cut:

- 2 strips, each 1½" x 42" (10 total), for the blocks

From the lightest of the ⅛-yd. solids, cut:

- 2 strips, each 2" x 42", for the blocks

From the mottled turquoise print, cut:

- 12 squares, each 6¾" x 6¾", for the blocks

From the yellow solid, cut:

- 24 regular and 24 reverse E pieces for stars

From the light blue denim, cut:

- 12 regular and 12 reverse D pieces for blocks
- 48 template I for inner sashing

From the dark blue denim, cut:

- 2 strips, each 1½" x 56½", for the top and bottom inner borders
- 2 strips, each 1½" x 74½", for the side inner borders
- 48 H pieces for outer sashing
- 1 square, 21" x 21", for the binding

X Marks the Spot, 67" x 85", by Georgia J. Bonesteel and Genevieve Grundy.

Assembling the Blocks

1. Join 2 A strips to the long edges of a B strip as shown. Make 12 and label them Unit 1.

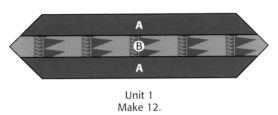

Unit 1
Make 12.

2. Sew together 6 beige-to–terra cotta strips to form a strip set. Place the 2"-wide (lightest) strip on an outer edge, and grade the remaining 5 strips from light to dark and back again. Repeat to make a second, identical strip set.

3. Use template C to cut 24 strips from the strip set as shown, positioning the template with its pointed end over the 2"-wide (lightest) strip.

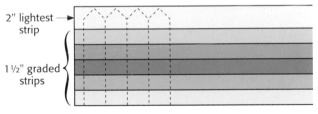

2" lightest strip

1½" graded strips

Make 2 strip sets.
Cut 24 of piece C.

4. Sew together the light blue regular D and yellow E pieces in pairs. Make 24 pairs. Repeat to sew the reverse D and E pieces into pairs. Press the seams in opposite directions.

5. Sew together a regular and a reverse pair, stopping and backstitching ¼" from the inside angle as shown. Press the seam open.

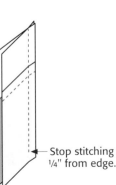

Stop stitching ¼" from edge.

6. Sew the pointed end of a pieced C strip to the inside angle of each D-E unit, pivoting at the point.

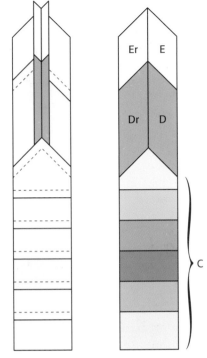

Er | E

Dr | D

C

Make 24.

7. Sew regular and reverse F strips to each pieced unit as shown. Press the seam allowances away from the pieced unit. Make 24 units and label them Unit 2.

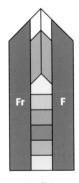

Fr | F

Unit 2
Make 24.

8. Cut each 6¾" turquoise square in half twice diagonally to make 48 quarter-square G triangles. Sew G triangles to opposite sides of Unit 2, sewing along a short edge of each triangle and aligning the bottom edges as shown. Stop stitching approximately 1" from the tops of the triangles.

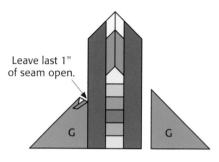

Leave last 1" of seam open.

9. Sew a Unit 2 to opposite sides of a Unit 1 as shown.

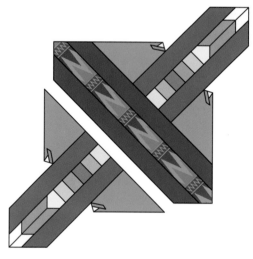

10. Stitch a dark blue H strip to the longest edge of a light blue I strip to make a pieced sashing strip. Make 48.

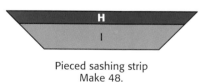

Pieced sashing strip
Make 48.

11. Sew H-I sashing strips to the corners of each block as shown, stopping ¼" from the corner. Finish the diagonal seams, then stitch the mitered sashing seams to finish the block. Repeat for all 12 blocks.

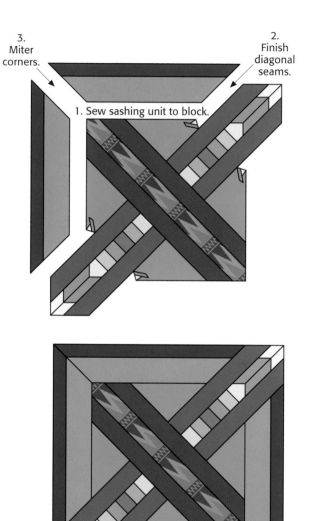

3.
Miter corners.

2.
Finish diagonal seams.

1. Sew sashing unit to block.

Finished block

Assembling the Quilt Top

1. Lay out the blocks in 4 horizontal rows of 3 blocks each, referring to the illustration to be certain you are positioning the blocks correctly. Sew the blocks into horizontal rows, then join the rows.

2. Add the 1½"-wide dark blue inner borders to the appropriate sides of the quilt and miter the corners. Repeat to add and miter the 6"-wide Southwestern print outer border.

Quilting and Finishing

1. Remove the selvages and piece the backing panels to make a single 83½" x 90" seamed backing. Center the batting and quilt top over the backing, and baste.

2. Quilt as desired. The sample was quilted with a combination of hand and machine quilting. A longer-than-usual stitch, done with brown buttonhole thread and a jeans needle, highlights the dark blue sashing and inner borders.

3. Cut the 21" dark blue square into 1¼"-wide bias strips for single-fold binding. Bind the quilt to finish.

Cover Lovers

The whimsical nature of the small quilts in this section
sets them apart from their more conventional relations.
More significant for me, however, is that "Cover Lovers" is the
name of a longstanding quilt group that originated from a class
I taught more than fifteen years ago. Where did the name
come from? A Southern expression for quilts is "kivers,"
but we couldn't call our group the "Kiver Livers,"
so we more appropriately became the Cover Lovers!

Round and Round We Go

How simple, how original, how practical can you get? I spotted this small quilt at our local curb market, where everything from vegetables to flowers to crafts is sold. The maker is LaVon Gilbert of Hendersonville, North Carolina, and her comment when interviewed was, "Well, I've just been making them for a long time."

Inspired, I wrote instructions for this darling quilt—updated, of course, for the sewing machine. Gather your leftovers, start cutting, and be prepared to stitch round and round.

Materials

(44"-WIDE FABRIC)

♦ 3¾ yds. *total* of assorted scrap fabrics (to total 76 running yds. of 2"-wide strips)*
♦ 32½" x 42½" rectangle of fabric for backing
♦ 30½" x 40½" rectangle of batting

*Yes, 76 yards is correct! See "Assembling the Quilt" below for an explanation of this unusual yardage.

Assembling the Quilt

1. Cut all the scrap fabric into 2"-wide strips, then stitch the strips end to end into 1 continuous strip that measures 76 yards long. That may seem like a lot of fabric, but keep in mind that the strip is narrow and scrappy, and that this long folded strip makes the entire quilt!

2. Fold the long strip wrong sides together and press.

3. Center the batting on the wrong side of the backing fabric, allowing the backing to extend 1" beyond the edge on all sides. Turn the excess backing fabric onto the batting and hand baste it in place, "mitering" the corners.

4. With a fabric marker and yardstick, trace a line from each corner toward the center of the batting as shown, being certain to mark each line at a 45-degree angle. Use a right-angle triangle or a ruler with a 45-degree angle marked on it to position the yardstick. In addition, mark a line along each edge of the batting, ⅜" from the raw edge of the backing "hem."

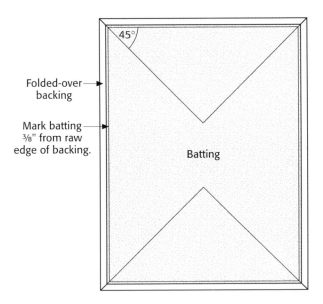

Round and Round We Go, 30½" x 40½", by LaVon Gilbert.

5. Thread your sewing machine with neutral-colored thread on top, and with thread to match the backing in the bobbin.

6. Starting along a straight edge (not at a corner), align the raw edge of the long strip with the ⅜" line drawn on the batting. The folded edge of the strip should face the outer edge of the quilt and overlap the raw edge of the turned-over backing.

7. Angle the raw edge of the folded strip in toward the center. Beginning approximately 3" from the end, stitch the strip to the batting and backing, using a blind hemstitch. To stitch, turn back the folded edge of the strip approximately ¼", and position the needle so that the straight stitches run along the folded back edge and a zigzag stitch just catches the strip every 3 stitches. (It is also possible to do this by hand with a long needle, taking small stitches to secure all the layers.)

8. Proceed around the perimeter of the quilt, folding mitered corners at the diagonal lines marked on the batting. Work toward the quilt's center, overlapping rows and using the folded edge of each new row to overlap the raw edge of the previous row by approximately ⅜" to ½". It will take about 34 continuous rows to fill the quilt from the outer edge to the center.

9. Finish the quilt—and cover the raw end of the strip—by appliquéing a ½"-wide (finished size) strip over the center. Whipstitch the outer fold to the backing fabric.

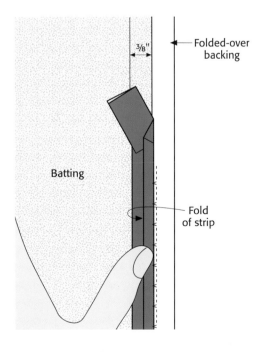

⅜"

Folded-over backing

Batting

Fold of strip

❦ Itsy Bitsy Spider ❧

When the decor for a baby's room originates with insect fabric, what sort of quilt can you make? A spider quilt, of course! A new notion—fusible bias tape—comes to the rescue for easy construction. Terri Bulk, all the way in Pennsylvania, completed this quilt from my instructions. She later wrote: "The bias tape–double-needle operation was slick . . . much easier than I had anticipated. What a clever idea!"

Materials

(44"-WIDE FABRIC)

- 36" x 48" rectangle of bright green solid or subtle print for background
- Assorted scraps for web sections
- 15 yds. of ½"-wide black fusible bias tape
- 1½ yds. fabric for backing
- Crib-size batting (45" x 60")
- 1 square, 22" x 22" for binding
- Gluestick

Drawing the Pattern

1. On a 36" x 48" piece of paper, use a yardstick to mark lines that divide it in half both horizontally and vertically. Draw 2 diagonal lines radiating at 45-degree angles from the center lines as shown.

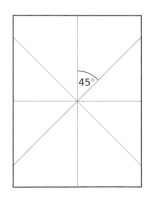

2. Beginning close to the center, use a flexicurve (page 11) to draw curved lines that connect the straight ones. Work out from the center to make 5 radiating rows for the web. Refer to the photo on page 79 for guidance.

3. Label the rows as shown on page 80, beginning with row A closest to the center and progressing to row E at the outer edge. Label the web sections as well, beginning with section 1 in the upper right-hand corner and working clockwise until you reach section 8 in the upper left.

Itsy Bitsy Spider, 36" x 48", by Georgia J. Bonesteel and Terri Bulk.

4. Designate 4 sections in each row with the letter *S*, for scrap. You will have a total of 20 scrap sections. Alternate the placement of the scrap sections from row to row as shown. The scrap sections are the only ones for which you will need to make templates.

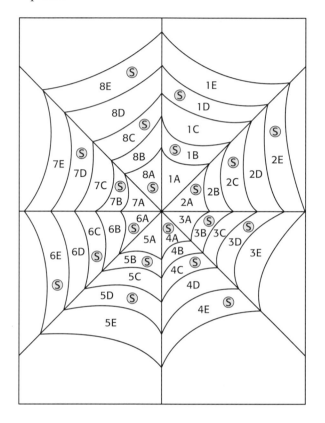

5. Tracing from your full-size drawing, mark the 20 scrap-section (S) templates onto freezer paper or Grid-Grip (page 110). Do not add seam allowances. Be sure to label each template with the appropriate letter and number.

Cutting and Assembling the Spiderweb

1. Press the freezer-paper templates onto the right sides of randomly selected scrap fabrics, and cut the web sections. Do not add seam allowances.

2. Use a fabric marker to draw the vertical, horizontal, and diagonal guidelines of the spiderweb onto the 36" x 48" rectangle of green background fabric. Refer to the full-size drawing and pin the row A scrap sections in place, using the straight lines as a guide. Remove the paper templates, and use a touch of gluestick to secure the scrap sections to the background. Do the same for the scrap sections in row B.

3. Following the manufacturer's instructions, press the fusible bias tape over the curved boundaries between rows A and B. There are 2 ways to stitch the bias tape to the quilt. You can install a double needle (4.0) on your sewing machine, use 2 spools of thread on top, and secure the bias tape by stitching it to the scrap fabric and the background (see "Needles" on page 10). If you don't have or can't install a double needle, simply stitch along each side of the tape a scant ⅛" from the edge. Add rows C through E in the same manner.

4. Finish the web by machine stitching the bias tape over the horizontal, vertical, and diagonal lines.

Quilting and Finishing

1. Center the quilt top and batting over the backing, and baste.

2. Quilt as desired—you might want to accent the web sections with outline quilting. Make your own rendition of a fuzzy spider to crawl into the center of the web.

3. Cut the 22" square of fabric into 2½"-wide strips for binding. There is enough fabric to cut strips on the straight of grain or bias, whichever you prefer. Bind the quilt to finish.

⇨ Button Up! ⇦

The secret stitches of "Button Up!" are the result of my search for innovative ways to connect quilted blocks. Made in holiday fabric, this quilt is the perfect seasonal lap throw. What a great idea for a baby quilt, too—just be sure to secure the fold-over scallops with stitching rather than buttons.

Finished Block Size: 12"

Materials
(44"- WIDE FABRIC)

NOTE: *"Button Up!" is a two-sided quilt, and the fabrics listed below include yardage for both the front and back.*

- 1¾ yds. *each* of a green print, a red print, a red plaid, and a red-and-green holiday print for blocks
- 50" x 62" piece of batting
- 81 red buttons
- 81 green buttons

Cutting

All measurements include ¼"-wide seam allowances.

1. You'll need to make a template to cut the blocks for this quilt. Draw a 12" square on graph paper and trace the scalloped border pattern on page 84 along all 4 sides. Transfer the pattern to your preferred template material and cut out the template.

2. Use the template to cut 10 scalloped blocks from each of the 4 block fabrics (green and red prints, red plaid, and holiday print). You'll have a total of 40 blocks, 20 for the front and 20 for the back.

3. From the batting, cut 20 squares, each 12" x 12".

Assembling the Blocks

1. Pair the 40 blocks, right sides together, as follows:
   - 5 plaid with 5 green print
   - 5 plaid with 5 red print
   - 5 holiday print with 5 green print
   - 5 holiday print with 5 red print

2. Pinch the corner of each block to lightly crease its diagonal midpoint. Use these creases to center a 12" square of batting on the wrong side of 1 block in each pair. Baste the batting in place by hand, stitching a scant ¼" from the edge of the square.

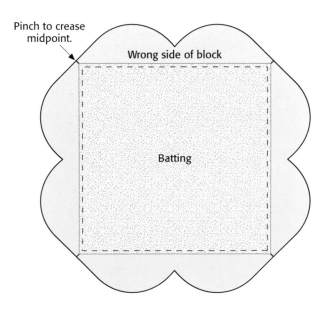

Pinch to crease midpoint.

Wrong side of block

Batting

Button Up!, 60" x 48", by Georgia J. Bonesteel, quilted by Georgia J. Bonesteel and friends.

3. Re-pair the fabric blocks, right sides together. Using a ¼"-wide seam allowance, machine stitch around the outer, scalloped edge of each pair, leaving a 3" to 4" opening along 1 side for turning. Trim any excess seam allowance on the outside curves, and clip *almost* to the stitching line at each inner pivot point.

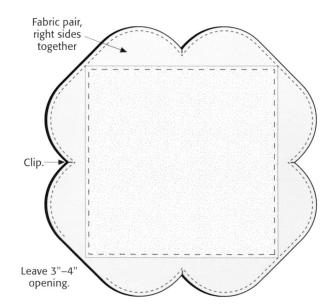

Fabric pair, right sides together

Clip.

Leave 3"–4" opening.

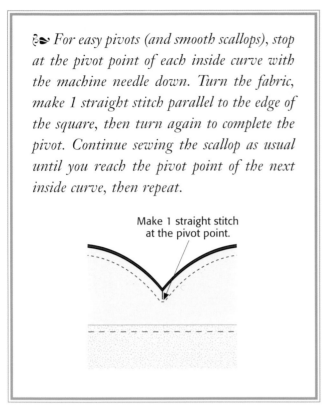

For easy pivots (and smooth scallops), stop at the pivot point of each inside curve with the machine needle down. Turn the fabric, make 1 straight stitch parallel to the edge of the square, then turn again to complete the pivot. Continue sewing the scallop as usual until you reach the pivot point of the next inside curve, then repeat.

Make 1 straight stitch at the pivot point.

4. Turn the block right side out. Maneuver your fingers inside the block to smooth the scallops, then press the block. Close the opening with a whipstitch. Repeat to complete all 20 blocks.

Assembling and Finishing the Quilt

1. Baste the block layers to secure them. Quilt each block with the holly leaf motifs on page 84 or as desired, taking care to stay within the 12" center square.

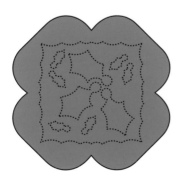

2. Remove the basting threads. Referring to the photo on page 82 and to the illustration on page 84, place the blocks in a balanced, pleasing arrangement of 4 horizontal rows of 5 blocks each. Some of the scallops fold over from the back of the quilt to the front, and vice versa, so keep this in mind as you arrange the blocks.

3. Position a 12" square ruler (or template) in the center of each block. Using a chalk marker, trace around the ruler to mark the center square, and repeat on the opposite side of the block. These marks are stitching lines for joining the blocks.

4. Pin 2 blocks together, both with right sides up, overlapping the scalloped edges as shown. Align the stitching lines, then sew along the line marked on the upper block. Assemble the blocks into rows, then join the rows.

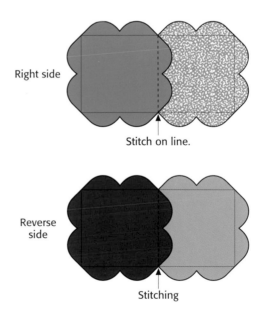

Right side

Stitch on line.

Reverse side

Stitching

5. Fold 2 opposite-side scallops inward over each block and pin in place, alternating side, then top and bottom scallops from block to block. Repeat for the back of the quilt.

6. Stitch a button to the middle of each scallop (2 per flap).

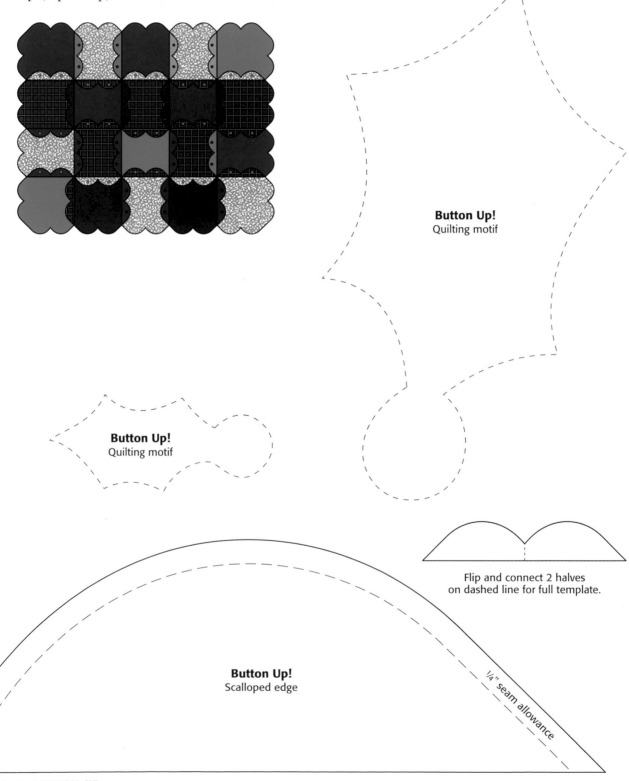

Button Up!
Quilting motif

Button Up!
Quilting motif

Button Up!
Scalloped edge

Flip and connect 2 halves
on dashed line for full template.

¼" seam allowance

❧ Christmas Wreath ❧

Quilters just love to decorate with patchwork during the holidays, and "Christmas Wreath" will generate seasonal cheer for years to come. A unique "inversion" technique adds a hanging tube in the final step and eliminates the need for binding.

Finished Block Size: 22"

Materials

(44"-WIDE FABRIC)

- 1¼ yds. white-on-white print for background
- 6 red and 6 green Christmas-print scraps for wreath
- ⅛ yd. red for inner border
- ⅛ yd. green for outer border
- 28" x 28" square of batting
- ⅞ yd. fabric for backing

Cutting

MAKE templates for pieces A through I by transferring the patterns on pages 88–89 and on the pullout to your preferred template material. Label each template with the appropriate letter, grainline arrows, and midpoint markers. All template and cutting measurements include ¼" seam allowances.

From the white-on-white print, cut:

- 1 I piece for background
- 24 A pieces for background
- 4 *each* of pieces C, D, E, F, G, and H for background
- 1 strip, 4" x 25½", for the hanging sleeve

From *each* of the 6 red and 6 green Christmas scraps, cut:

- 2 B pieces for wreath

From the red border fabric, cut:

- 2 strips, each 1¼" x 22½", for the side inner borders
- 2 strips, each 1¼" x 23¾", for the top and bottom inner borders

From the green border fabric, cut:

- 2 strips, each 1½" x 23¾", for the side outer borders
- 2 strips, each 1½" x 25¾", for the top and bottom outer borders

Assembling the Quilt

1. Arrange the pieces as shown, placing the B triangles in a color-balanced circle.

Christmas Wreath, 25¼" x 25¼", by Georgia J. Bonesteel.

2. Stitch an A piece to the inner short edge of each B triangle as shown.

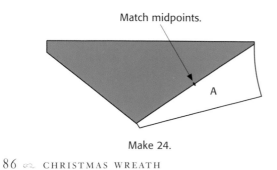

Match midpoints.

A

Make 24.

3. Finish 4 wedges by sewing a C piece to the short outer edge of the appropriate A-B unit. Complete the remaining A-B units in sets of 4 by adding D, E, F, G, and H pieces.

4. Sew 6 wedges together to form a quarter of the wreath. Make 4 quarters, join the quarters to make 2 halves, and then join the halves to complete the wreath. Fold the wreath into quarters and mark the midpoints at the edges.

5. Fold the I circle into quarters and mark the midpoints at the edges. Pin the circle to the pieced wreath, right sides together, matching the midpoint markings. Sew the pieces together, easing gently as needed.

> ❧ *You'll find it easier to stitch the circle if you match the quarter sections of the pieced wreath and the I circle, pin, and hand baste in place. Finish by machine stitching with the pieced wreath on top and the I circle against the feed dogs.*

6. Sew the 1¼"-wide red side borders to the quilt top, then add the top and bottom borders. Repeat to add the 1½"-wide green outer borders.

Match quarter marks.

Quilting and Finishing

1. Turn under ¼" on the short raw edges of the 4" x 25½" strip and stitch to finish. Fold the strip right sides out, aligning the long raw edges. This will be the hanging sleeve for your quilt.

2. Layer the quilt top (right side up), the sleeve, and the quilt backing (wrong side up), carefully aligning the top raw edges. Place the batting on top, again aligning the raw edges, and generously pin: then baste.

3. Flip the sandwich over so that the wrong side of the quilt top faces you and the batting rests against the feed dogs of your sewing machine. Stitch completely around all 4 sides, using a ¼" seam allowance.

4. Taking extra care to avoid cutting the quilt top, slit a 3" opening through the batting and backing, near the top edge where the slit will be covered by the sleeve. Remove the pins, turn the quilt right side out, and whipstitch the opening closed. Staystitch (or "set") the edges with a row of machine stitching, then baste.

5. Quilt as desired, then whipstitch the bottom edge of the sleeve in place. Insert a narrow, 25"-long wooden lattice strip, and your "Christmas Wreath" is ready for hanging.

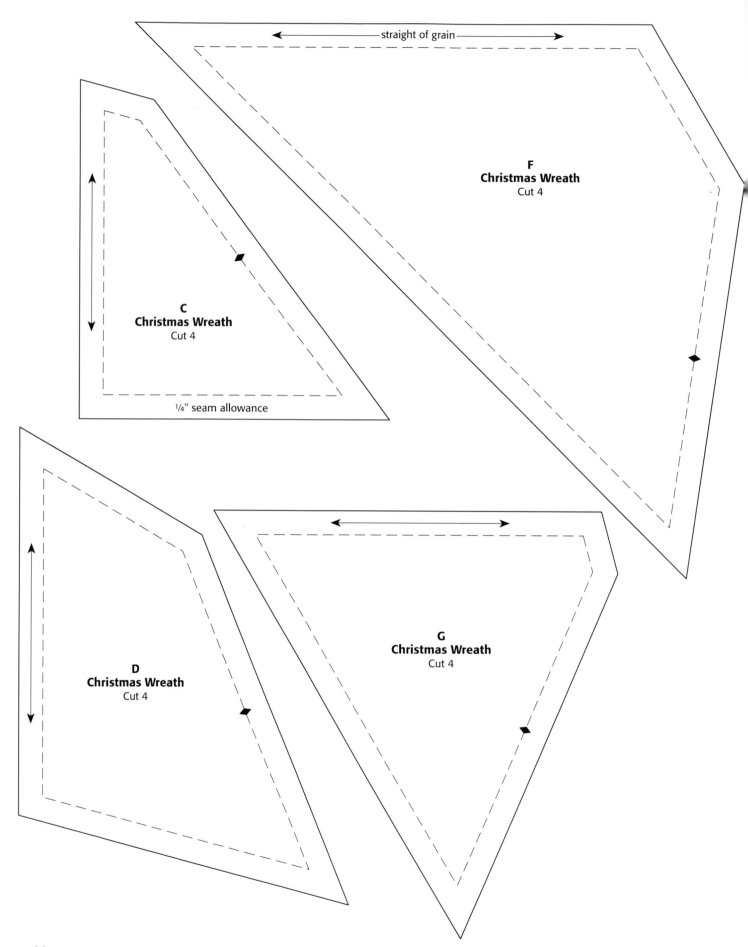

straight of grain

F
Christmas Wreath
Cut 4

C
Christmas Wreath
Cut 4

¼" seam allowance

D
Christmas Wreath
Cut 4

G
Christmas Wreath
Cut 4

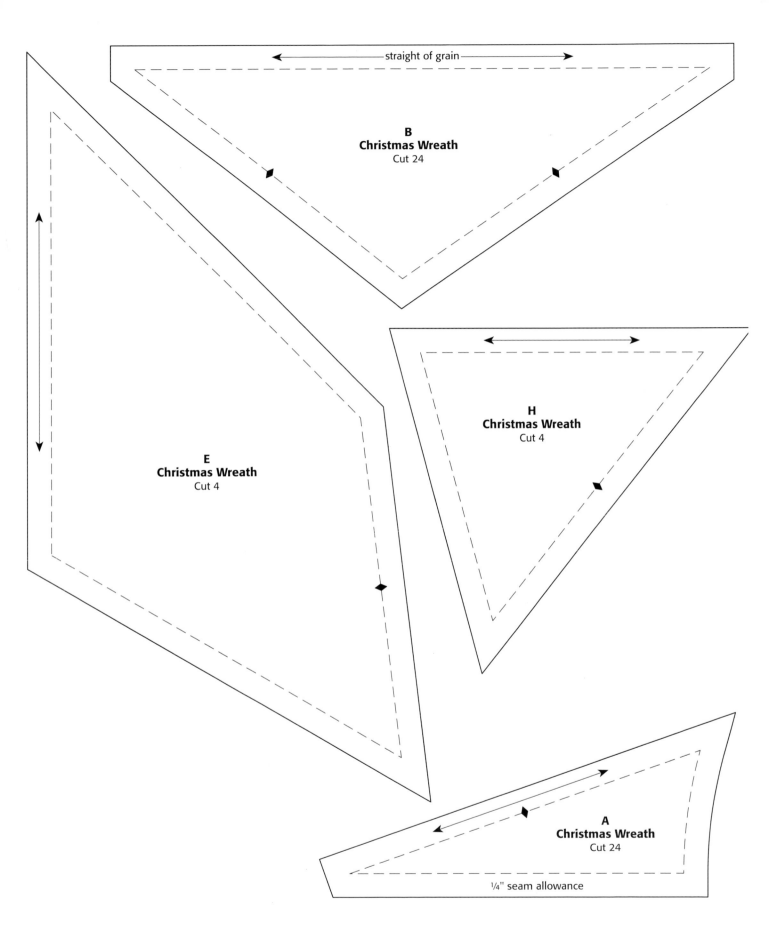

straight of grain

B
Christmas Wreath
Cut 24

H
Christmas Wreath
Cut 4

E
Christmas Wreath
Cut 4

A
Christmas Wreath
Cut 24

¼" seam allowance

Flip-flop Diamonds

With a niece in Hong Kong to provide the silk, and inspiration from Hanne Vieke DeKoning, a Dutch quilter whose specialty is silk patchwork, I made Flip-flop Diamonds. Patchwork and silk was a foreign combination to me, but just a few alterations in technique made it possible. A magazine ad for a woolen rug provided the original design inspiration.

Materials
(44"-WIDE FABRIC)

- ⅞ yd. black silk for patchwork and outer borders
- 10" x 32" rectangle of purple silk for patchwork and inner side border
- 8" x 42" rectangle of green silk for patchwork and inner side border
- 18" x 28" rectangle of red silk for patchwork and inner bottom border
- 15" x 28" rectangle of gold silk for patchwork and inner top border
- 10" x 28" rectangle of plaid silk #1 for patchwork and corner triangles
- 22" x 22" square of plaid silk #2 for binding
- 1¼ yds. permanent, iron-on knit stabilizer
- 33" x 64½" piece of batting
- 1⅞ yds. fabric for backing

Preparing to Cut

1. Following the manufacturer's instructions, press stabilizer to the back of all the silk but the 22" square. Use a pressing cloth to avoid damaging the fabric.

2. Make templates for pieces A through E by transferring the patterns on the pullout to your preferred template material. Label each template with the appropriate letter and grain-line arrows.

Cutting

All measurements include ¼"-wide seam allowances.

From the black silk, cut:

♦ 4 strips, each 2" x 42", for the outer borders

♦ 14 A pieces

♦ 4 B pieces

From the purple silk, cut:

♦ 1 strip, 1¼" x 22", for the inner side border

♦ 6 A pieces

♦ 4 B pieces

From the green silk, cut:

♦ 1 strip, 1¼" x 22", for the inner side border

♦ 8 A pieces

From the red silk, cut:

♦ 2 strips, each 1¼" x 28", for the inner bottom border

♦ 8 A pieces

♦ 8 C pieces

From the gold silk, cut:

♦ 2 strips, each 1¼" x 28", for the inner top border

♦ 2 regular and 2 reverse D pieces

♦ 6 regular and 6 reverse E pieces

From plaid silk #1, cut:

♦ 6 A pieces

♦ 4 B pieces

♦ 6 C pieces

♦ 2 squares, each 5" x 5", for the corner triangles

Flip-flop Diamonds, 54" x 21½", by Georgia J. Bonesteel.

Assembling the Quilt

1. Lay out the pieces as shown below, then stitch them into 8 horizontal rows. Set your iron on a medium setting and use a pressing cloth to press the seam allowances open. Join the rows to complete the center of the quilt top.

2. Sew together the four 2" x 42" black silk strips to make 1 continuous 2"-wide strip (see the tip box on page 24). From this single long strip, cut 2 outer side borders, each 22" long, and an outer top and bottom border, each 54½" long. In a similar fashion, piece the two 1¼" x 28" red strips and the two 1¼" x 28" gold strips, and cut each to a length of 54½", for the inner top and bottom borders.

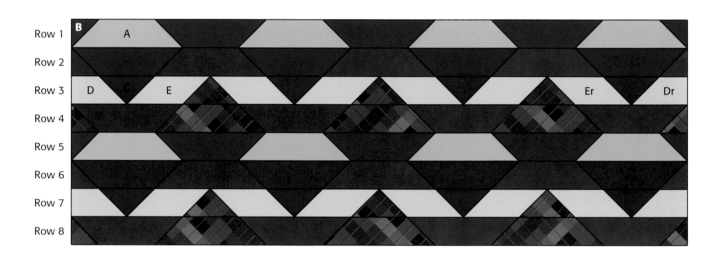

3. Stitch each red, gold, purple, and green inner border strip to a black silk outer border strip of matching length to make a total of 4 border units. Matching ends and midpoints, pin and stitch the appropriate border unit to each side of the quilt, referring to the photo on page 91 to be certain you are positioning the strips correctly (black to the outside). Don't worry about finishing the corners; just stitch to the raw edge of the quilt top.

4. Cut each 5" plaid square in half diagonally for a total of 4 half-square border triangles. Position a triangle wrong side up on the quilt top, with the point toward the center as shown. Pin, then stitch along the edge of the triangle, taking the usual ¼" seam. Repeat for the remaining corners. Trim the excess border strips, then flip back the corner triangles and press them in place, squaring the corners of the quilt with a ruler if necessary.

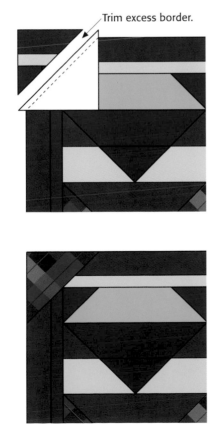

Trim excess border.

Quilting and Finishing

1. Center the batting and quilt top over the backing, and baste.

2. Quilt as desired. In the sample, novelty stitches cover some of the key seams.

3. Cut the 22" square of unstabilized plaid silk into 2½"-wide bias binding strips, and bind the quilt to finish.

Flora and Fauna

Flora, fauna, and good old Mother Nature can always
find places in the quilting world. Picture quilts make
charming patchwork projects, and they present
all sorts of fun possibilities.

◄ The Jersey Cow Quilt ▷

What to do when the request for a Jersey cow quilt came to the Landrum (SC) Quilters Guild? I finally broke the silence at the monthly meeting by volunteering, "Yes, we can do it!" What I especially liked was the goal for completion: the annual meeting of the American Jersey Cattle Association in the year 2000.

Finished Block Size: 10"

Materials
(44"-WIDE FABRIC)

- 3 yds. medium brown solid or subtle print for cow heads
- Assorted dark brown solid or subtle-print scraps for cow ears and eyes
- 4 yds. *total* of assorted blue fabrics for block backgrounds
- 2½ yds. medium green solid or subtle print for sashing and hills on bottom border
- 2½ yds *total* of assorted blue scraps, of varying values, for the pieced borders
- ¼ yd. *total* of assorted yellow scraps for top border
- 3¼ yds. lightweight foundation for border panels*
- 9½ yds. fabric for backing
- 33" x 33" square of fabric for binding
- King-size batting (120" x 120")
- 10" x 32¾" rectangle of freezer-paper for sunburst foundation

*Loosely woven, inexpensive muslin makes a good foundation.

Cutting

MAKE templates for pieces A, B, C, D, E, and F by transferring the patterns on the pullout to your preferred template material. Label each template by letter, and include the grain-line arrows. In addition, transfer the character lines (eyes, mouth, neck wrinkles, etc.) and ear and eye placement guidelines to template A, and to the fabric when cutting the A pieces.

All measurements include ¼"-wide seam allowances.

From the medium brown fabric, cut:

- 26 regular and 26 reverse A pieces for cow heads

From the dark brown scraps, cut:

- 52 regular and 52 reverse C pieces (in matching pairs) for ears
- 52 regular and 52 D reverse pieces (in matching pairs) for ears
- 52 E for eyes

From the assorted blue fabrics, cut:

- 26 regular and 26 B reverse pieces for block backgrounds

From the green fabric, cut:

- 2 strips, each 1½" x 87½", for the top and bottom sashing
- 60 strips, each 1½" x 10½", for the vertical sashing
- 7 strips, each 1½" x 67½", for the horizontal sashing
- 5 strips, each 6" x 18", for the hills

From the foundation fabric, cut:

- 1 panel, 11" x 66", for the bottom border
- 4 panels, each 11" x 50", for the side borders

The Jersey Cow Quilt, 87" x 109", by Georgia J. Bonesteel and the Landrum Quilters Guild,
quilted by Zula Hughey and Georgia J. Bonesteel .

Assembling the Cow Blocks

1. Place matching C regular and reverse ears right sides together. Using a ¼" seam allowance, stitch around the curvy edge only—leave the bottom (straight) edge open. The unstitched edge will be caught in the seam when the block is assembled. Turn the ear right side out. Make 52 C ears.

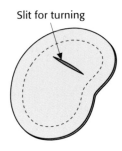

Leave open to turn.

2. Place matching D regular and reverse ears right sides together and stitch, this time completing the seam all around the ear shape. On the back of the ear, carefully cut a small slit near the bottom edge and turn the ear right side out. Make 52 D ears.

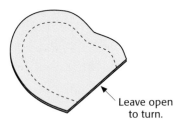

Slit for turning

3. Place a matching A head and B sky backgrounds (both regular or both reverse) right sides together. Fold over the curved end of a C ear, then insert the ear between the 2 pieces where indicated on the pattern, aligning the raw edges. The fold should face the cow fabric. Join the 2 pieces, pinning each angled segment as you go. Clip all obtuse angles almost to the seam line, then sew the pieces together. (If your sewing machine has an automatic "needle-down" feature, use it as you stitch to make pivoting easier.) Press the seams whichever way they want to go. Make 52 cow blocks.

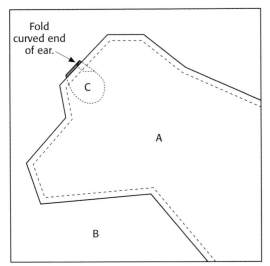

Fold curved end of ear.

C

A

B

4. Appliqué a D ear on each cow head, placing the ear as indicated on the pattern. Leave the upper edge free for a 3-dimensional touch. Appliqué an eye (piece E) on each cow.

5. Machine or hand embroider the details on the cow heads with black thread.

> *Here are some tips for successful machine embroidery, or "thread sketching":*
>
> - *Use a contrasting thread color.*
> - *Tighten the tension on the bobbin thread.*
> - *Drop the feed dogs.*
> - *Set your sewing machine for a narrow zigzag stitch.*
> - *Use a narrow hoop to hold the fabric taut.*
> - *Add depth by making repeated, side-by-side lines of stitching.*
> - *Avoid stabilizers, which can distort stitches when removed and add unwanted bulk.*

6. Since there are 52 cow blocks in the quilt—and since the quilt was made for a national organization—our group did some research. We appliquéd a state-flower wreath around the neck of each cow and machine embroidered the state name under each chin. From Alabama to Wyoming—plus the District of Columbia—each cow is decorated. Do some research of your own, and use your imagination to appliqué, embroider, or otherwise embellish the cows. The fifty-second block can be your signature block.

   We embroidered two-letter state postal abbreviations on the blocks, then arranged them in alphabetical order. If you want to do the same, be sure that each cow faces the right direction when you label it. The upper left-hand border cow is Alaska (AK) and the lower right is Wyoming (WY). The cows in the horizontal rows are labeled alphabetically for the states in between. The upper right cow represents our nation's capital (DC), and the lower left cow is unlabeled.

Making the Pieced Borders

1. From the assorted blue fabrics, cut 22 regular and 22 reverse F pieces, and 2 squares, each 11" x 11"; cut the squares once diagonally.

2. Begin by placing a triangle at 1 end of an 11" x 50" side foundation strip as shown. Place 1 regular F piece on the triangle, right sides together, then stitch. Add a total of 11 regular F pieces to cover the muslin foundation. Repeat with 11 reverse pieces to make a mirror-image border section. Make 2 of each border section. Trim the sections to 10½" x 44½" as shown.

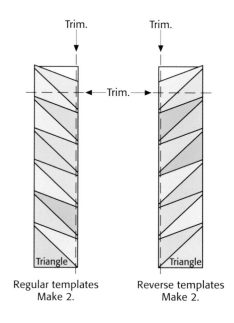

Regular templates
Make 2.

Reverse templates
Make 2.

3. Join 2 mirror-image sections at the large triangle to make each of the side borders.

4. The top border (with sunburst) is made with the aid of a 10" x 32¾" paper pattern cut from Grid-Grip or freezer paper (see "Materials" on page 95). One 10" end of the rectangular panel represents the center of the border.

   Make all markings on the dull side of the paper. Measure and mark 5" up from the bottom left corner along the left side of the paper panel. Measure and mark the long bottom edge of the panel approximately 17" from the left bottom corner. Use a flexicurve (see page 11) to draw a gentle curve connecting the points as shown.

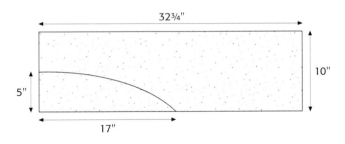

   Use a ruler to draw 10 radiating lines, and label the sections 1through 11 and "blue" and "yellow" as shown on the coded diagram. Cut out the templates.

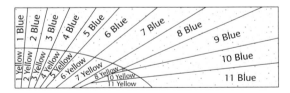

5. Pair 2 like-colored (blue) scraps right sides together. The scraps may be the same or different fabrics. With a dry iron set on the cotton setting, press a sky template shiny side down on the top fabric in the pair. Repeat with different pairs of blue scraps for all 11 blue (sky) templates. Leave the paper template in place, and use a rotary cutter and gridded ruler to cut around each template, adding an accurate ¼" seam allowance.

6. Repeat Step 5 to cut 11 pairs of yellow scraps.

7. Stitch matching (blue #1 and yellow #1; blue #2 and yellow #2, etc.) pieces in pairs, removing the paper templates as you go. You'll have 2 sets of blue-yellow mirror-image wedges, numbered 1–11. Press seam allowances in opposite directions.

   Starting with the center (#1) wedge, stitch the wedges together to make 2 mirror-image border panels. Press as you go. Join the 2 panels at the center seam and press.

8. Cut 6" x 12" strips from the assorted blue fabrics for the bottom border; fold or layer your fabrics so that you cut the strips in matching pairs. Working from the center out on the remaining 11" x 66" foundation, stitch matching blue strips to opposite sides of the center strip, using the sew-and-flip method. Angle the strips as shown.

9. Fold each 6" x 18" green strip in half cross-wise and cut out a gentle curve. Appliqué the green hills along the bottom of the pieced foundation. Trim the bottom panel to 10½" x 65½".

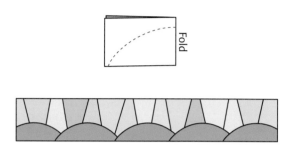

Assembling the Quilt Top

1. Arrange the cow blocks alphabetically in 8 horizontal rows of 6 blocks each (see step 6, page 98 for help with the arrangement). Place a 1½" x 10½" sashing strip between each block and along the outer edges. Join the blocks and sashing strips.

2. Place 1½" x 67½" sashing strips between each row. Join the horizontal rows and sashing strips, taking care to keep the vertical strips aligned. Add the 2 side pieced borders.

3. Sew 1½" x 87½" sashing strips to the top and bottom edges of the assembled blocks.

4. Stitch a 1½" x 10½" sashing strip and cow head to each short end of the top and bottom pieced borders. Stitch the borders in place to complete the quilt top.

Quilting and Finishing

1. Divide the backing fabric into 3 panels of equal length (114"), remove the selvages, then join along the selvage edges to make a single large backing. Trim the batting to approximately 91" x 112". Center the quilt top and batting over the seamed backing, and baste.

2. Quilt as desired. On the sample quilt, each cow is outline quilted.

3. Cut the 33" square of fabric into 2½"-wide strips for binding. There is enough fabric to cut strips on the straight of grain or bias, whichever you prefer. Bind the quilt to finish.

❧ Coast to Coast ❧

Quilted shells, waves, and seashore motifs surface against a background of ocean colors, from aqua to blue, while "secret stitches" hide beneath curved borders. The signature quilt for my tenth Lap Quilting series for public television, "Coast to Coast" represents our theme: From coast to coast, we visited quilt shops and explored what's new in quilt-making.

Finished Block Size: 18"

Materials

- 20 squares, each 22" x 22", of assorted ocean-colored (blue, green, and aqua) solids for the block fronts
- 10 squares, each 22" x 22", of assorted white-on-white prints for the block backs
- 10 squares, each 22" x 22", of assorted cream-on-muslin prints for the block backs
- 20 squares, each 18" x 18", of batting

Assembling the Blocks

1. You'll need to make a template to cut the blocks for this quilt. Draw an 18" square on graph paper and trace the scalloped border pattern on the pullout along all 4 sides. Be sure to mark a guideline arrow for cutting a slit in the finished block. Transfer the pattern to your preferred template material and cut out the template.

2. Make an 18" square template, drawing lines from corner to corner in both directions to mark the center.

3. Place an ocean-colored and a white (or cream) fabric square right sides together, aligning the raw edges. Center the curved template over the paired fabrics, trace, and cut. Repeat to trace and cut 20 pairs of curved blocks.

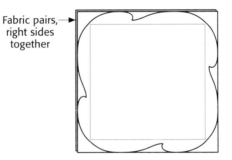

Fabric pairs, right sides together

4. Working 1 pair at a time, separate the 2 cut blocks. Center the 18" square template on the *right* side of the ocean-colored block, and trace. This square marks the sewing line for the "secret stitches" that will join the blocks.

   Mark the vertical and horizontal midpoints along the edges of the square, and lightly crease the block along both diagonals. Repeat for each of the 20 block pairs.

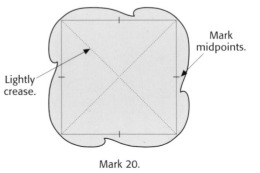

Mark midpoints.

Lightly crease.

Mark 20.

Coast to Coast, 72" x 90", by Georgia J. Bonesteel.

Quilt back

5. Transfer the desired quilting motif to each ocean-colored block, using the midpoints and creases to center the design within the 18" square. For the sample, I created 10 seashore patterns and 1 circular wave stencil for the quilting lines. The latter appears full-size on the pullout. See "Resources" on page 110 for information on ordering the full set of quilting patterns, or design your own!

6. Center the 18" square template on the *wrong* side of each ocean-colored block, and lightly trace around the corners. Center an 18" square of batting within these corner markings, and baste the batting in place.

7. Place each block pair right sides together, carefully aligning the curved edges. Stitch around the *entire outer edge* of the block, using a ¼" seam allowance (see the tip box on page 83 for hints on making painless pivots). Trim any excess seam allowance, and clip almost to the stitching line at the inside curves.

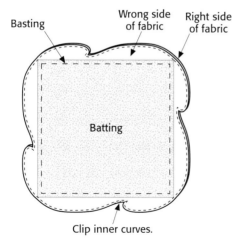

Basting

Wrong side of fabric

Right side of fabric

Batting

Clip inner curves.

8. For each block, carefully separate the 2 fabric layers. Cut the slit, as marked on the curve template, in the *top layer only*. Turn the block right side out, and whipstitch the slit closed.

9. Staystitch approximately ¼" from the outer edge of each block, working the edge with your fingers to distribute the fabric evenly.

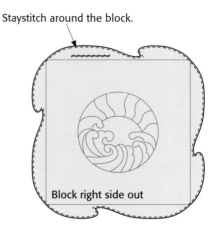

Staystitch around the block.

Block right side out

Wave detail

Quilting and Finishing

1. Baste the 3 layers of each block, and quilt the premarked motifs as desired.

2. Remove the basting threads and any visible quilt markings. Place the 20 quilted blocks in a balanced, pleasing arrangement of 5 horizontal rows of 4 blocks each, alternating white-backed and cream-backed blocks from block to block and row to row.

3. Place 2 blocks light sides together, aligning the marked stitching lines. (The curved edges will not match.) Pin, then stitch on the lines.

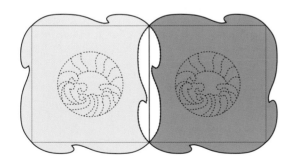

4. Hand stitch the wave edges to the block fronts.

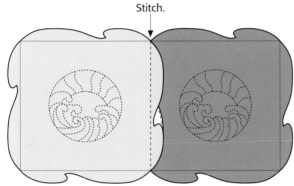

5. Complete each horizontal row by connecting the blocks and finishing the handwork. Join rows 1, 2, and 3; then rows 4 and 5, again finishing the handwork as you go. Complete the quilt by joining the 3-row and 2-row sections. Since there is no binding, you are ready to enjoy your finished quilt!

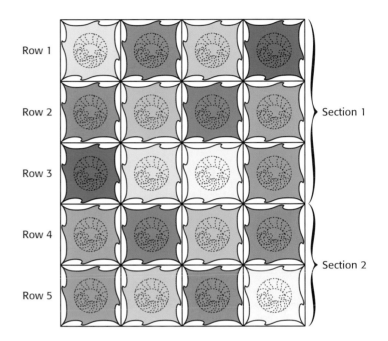

✒ Joe Cool and Company ✑

What is a quilt book without a cat pattern? Cats add contentment to my life with their "pieceful" manner. In fact, my days are not complete without my cat, PeeWee, nearby. However, watch out for the feline appetite. Cats like to eat cotton batting, so hide anything with exposed edges!

"Joe Cool and Company" was made by Janice Maddox of Asheville, North Carolina. She is an active member of the Asheville Quilt Guild and a teacher par excellence.

Materials

(44"-WIDE FABRIC)

- 1⅛ yds. dark blue cat print for blocks
- ⅞ yd. light multicolored cat print for blocks
- ½ yd. medium red cat print for border triangles
- ⅓ yd. yellow solid for binding
- 1¼ yds. fabric for backing
- 40" x 44" rectangle of batting

Cutting

All measurements include ¼"-wide seam allowances.

From the dark blue print, cut:

- 17 squares, each 4⅞" x 4⅞", for the blocks B, C, and D
- 24 squares, each 4½" x 4½", for the blocks A and E
- 30 squares, each 2½" x 2½", for the blocks C and D

From the light multicolored print, cut:

- 17 squares, each 4⅞" x 4⅞", for the blocks B, C, and D
- 13 squares, each 4½" x 4½", for the block A
- 30 squares, each 2½" x 2½", for the blocks C and E

From the medium red print, cut:

- 7 squares, each 6⅞" x 6⅞", for the border triangles

From the yellow solid, cut:

- 4 strips, each 2½" x 42", for the straight-grain binding

Joe Cool and Company, 34" x 39½", by Janice Maddox

Assembling the Blocks

"Joe Cool and Company" is a tessellating (interlocking) design. You'll need 5 different units to achieve the interlocking effect.

1. Pair a 4⅞" blue square with a 4⅞" light square, right sides together. Use a see-through gridded ruler to mark the top square in half along 1 diagonal.

2. Mark a line ¼" from each side of the diagonal line. Machine stitch directly on the 2 new lines.

3. Use a rotary cutter or scissors to cut on the original diagonal line. Open the 2 triangles, and press the seam toward the darker fabric. "Prune" the dog ears.

4. Repeat steps 1–3 to make a total of 34 half-square triangle B units. Set aside 4 units. The remaining B units will be used to construct other blocks.

Unit B
Make 34.

5. Place a 2½" blue square right sides together with a B unit, aligning a corner of the square with the right-angle corner of the light triangle. Mark the diagonal on the smaller square as shown, and sew directly on the line. Trim ¼" from the seam as shown and press toward the small corner triangle. Make 30 C units. Set aside 6 units. The remaining C units will be used to construct other blocks.

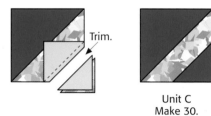

Trim.

Unit C
Make 30.

3. To make block D, stitch a 2½" light square to the opposite corner of the 24 remaining C units as shown.

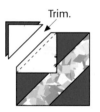

Trim.

Block D
Make 24.

4. To make block E, stitch a 2½" light square to the upper right corner of six 4½" blue squares as shown.

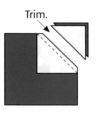

Trim.

Block E
Make 6.

Assembling the Quilt

1. Cut each of the 6⅞" red squares in half twice diagonally to make 28 setting triangles. (You'll have 2 left over.)

2. Lay out the quilt top as shown. Sew the blocks into diagonal rows, then join the rows, carefully matching the seams.

Quilting and Finishing

1. Center the quilt top and batting over the backing fabric, and baste.

2. Quilt as desired. The sample was stitched in a combination of free-motion and in-the-ditch machine quilting.

3. Piece the 2½"-wide binding strips to form a continuous, double-fold binding. Bind the quilt to finish.

Afterword

THE END OF a quilt book, I trust, is only the beginning of days filled with stitches. After writing seven books, I marvel at quiltmakers' continued exploration and all the fresh opportunities available for creativity.

My quilt world revolves around eager students, family, and home. Knowing that every quilt a student or viewer completes results in the gratification of the "look at me, I can do it," feeling, ribbons at quilt shows, gifts under Christmas trees, and beauty in the home makes my work very rewarding. Thank you for viewing my Lap Quilting television shows, and thank you for reading this book. Best wishes for small stitches.

—GEORGIA J. BONESTEEL

Resources

Photo-Transfer Methods

Bonsib, Sandy. *Quilting Your Memories: Inspirations for Designing with Image Transfers.* Bothell, Wash.: Martingale & Company, 1999.

To purchase Grid-Grip (gridded freezer paper) or "Coast to Coast" quilting templates, contact:

Lap Quilting
PO Box 96
Flat Rock, NC 28731
www.georgiabonesteel.com

❧ About the Author ❧

GEORGIA BONESTEEL is an internationally known TV personality and quilt-book author who has introduced thousands to the joys of quiltmaking. She has hosted her own PBS series, *Lap Quilting with Georgia Bonesteel*, for more than ten years.

Books from Martingale & Company

Appliqué
Appliqué in Bloom
Baltimore Bouquets
Basic Quiltmaking Techniques for Hand Appliqué
Basic Quiltmaking Techniques for Machine Appliqué
Coxcomb Quilt
The Easy Art of Appliqué
Folk Art Animals
From a Quilter's Garden
Fun with Sunbonnet Sue
Garden Appliqué
Interlacing Borders
Once Upon a Quilt
Stars in the Garden
Sunbonnet Sue All Through the Year
Welcome to the North Pole

Basic Quiltmaking Techniques
Basic Quiltmaking Techniques for Borders & Bindings
Basic Quiltmaking Techniques for Curved Piecing
Basic Quiltmaking Techniques for Divided Circles
Basic Quiltmaking Techniques for Eight-Pointed Stars
Basic Quiltmaking Techniques for Hand Appliqué
Basic Quiltmaking Techniques for Machine Appliqué
Basic Quiltmaking Techniques for Strip Piecing
Your First Quilt Book (or it should be!)

Crafts
15 Beads
The Art of Handmade Paper and Collage
Christmas Ribbonry
Fabric Mosaics
Folded Fabric Fun
Hand-Stitched Samplers from I Done My Best
The Home Decorator's Stamping Book
Making Memories
A Passion for Ribbonry
Stamp with Style

Design Reference
Color: The Quilter's Guide
Design Essentials: The Quilter's Guide
Design Your Own Quilts
The Nature of Design
QuiltSkills
Surprising Designs from Traditional Quilt Blocks

Foundation/Paper Piecing
Classic Quilts with Precise Foundation Piecing
Crazy but Pieceable
Easy Machine Paper Piecing
Easy Mix & Match Machine Paper Piecing
Easy Paper-Pieced Keepsake Quilts
Easy Paper-Pieced Miniatures
Easy Reversible Vests
Go Wild with Quilts
Go Wild with Quilts—Again!
It's Raining Cats & Dogs
Mariner's Medallion
Paper Piecing the Seasons
A Quilter's Ark
Sewing on the Line
Show Me How to Paper Piece

Home Decorating
Decorate with Quilts & Collections
The Home Decorator's Stamping Book
Living with Little Quilts
Make Room for Quilts
Special-Occasion Table Runners
Stitch & Stencil
Welcome Home: Debbie Mumm
Welcome Home: Kaffe Fassett

Joy of Quilting Series
Borders by Design
The Easy Art of Appliqué
A Fine Finish

Hand-Dyed Fabric Made Easy
Happy Endings
Loving Stitches
Machine Quilting Made Easy
A Perfect Match
Press for Success
Sensational Settings
Shortcuts
The Ultimate Book of Quilt Labels

Knitting
Simply Beautiful Sweaters
Two Sticks and a String
Welcome Home: Kaffe Fassett

Machine Quilting/Sewing
Machine Needlelace
Machine Quilting Made Easy
Machine Quilting with Decorative Threads
Quilting Makes the Quilt
Thread Magic
Threadplay

Miniature/Small Quilts
Celebrate! with Little Quilts
Crazy but Pieceable
Easy Paper-Pieced Miniatures
Fun with Miniature Log Cabin Blocks
Little Quilts All Through the House
Living with Little Quilts
Miniature Baltimore Album Quilts
Small Quilts Made Easy
Small Wonders

Quilting/Finishing Techniques
Borders by Design
The Border Workbook
A Fine Finish
Happy Endings
Interlacing Borders
Loving Stitches
Quilt It!
Quilting Design Sourcebook
Quilting Makes the Quilt
Traditional Quilts with Painless Borders
The Ultimate Book of Quilt Labels

Rotary Cutting/Speed Piecing
101 Fabulous Rotary-Cut Quilts
All-Star Sampler
Around the Block with Judy Hopkins
Bargello Quilts
Basic Quiltmaking Techniques for Strip Piecing
Block by Block
Easy Seasonal Wall Quilts
Easy Star Sampler
Fat Quarter Quilts
The Heirloom Quilt
The Joy of Quilting
More Quilts for Baby
More Strip-Pieced Watercolor Magic
A New Slant on Bargello Quilts
A New Twist on Triangles
Patchwork Pantry
Quilters on the Go
Quilting Up a Storm
Quilts for Baby
Quilts from Aunt Amy
ScrapMania
Simply Scrappy Quilts
Square Dance
Strip-Pieced Watercolor Magic
Stripples Strikes Again!
Strips That Sizzle
Two-Color Quilts

Seasonal Projects
Christmas Ribbonry
Easy Seasonal Wall Quilts

Folded Fabric Fun
Holiday Happenings
Quilted for Christmas
Quilted for Christmas, Book III
Quilted for Christmas, Book IV
A Silk-Ribbon Album
Welcome to the North Pole

Stitchery/Needle Arts
Christmas Ribbonry
Crazy Rags
Hand-Stitched Samplers from I Done My Best
Machine Needlelace
Miniature Baltimore Album Quilts
A Passion for Ribbonry
A Silk-Ribbon Album
Victorian Elegance

Surface Design/Fabric Manipulation
15 Beads
The Art of Handmade Paper and Collage
Complex Cloth
Creative Marbling on Fabric
Dyes & Paints
Hand-Dyed Fabric Made Easy
Jazz It Up

Theme Quilts
The Cat's Meow
Everyday Angels in Extraordinary Quilts
Fabric Collage Quilts
Fabric Mosaics
Folded Fabric Fun
Folk Art Quilts
Honoring the Seasons
It's Raining Cats & Dogs
Life in the Country with Country Threads
Making Memories
More Quilts for Baby
The Nursery Rhyme Quilt
Once Upon a Quilt
Patchwork Pantry
Quilted Landscapes
Quilting Your Memories
Quilts for Baby
Quilts from Nature
Through the Window and Beyond
Two-Color Quilts

Watercolor Quilts
More Strip-Pieced Watercolor Magic
Strip-Pieced Watercolor Magic
Watercolor Impressions
Watercolor Quilts

Wearables
Crazy Rags
Dress Daze
Easy Reversible Vests
Jacket Jazz Encore
Just Like Mommy
Variations in Chenille

Many of these books are available through your local quilt, fabric, craft-supply, or art-supply store. For more information, call, write, fax, or e-mail for our free full-color catalog.

Martingale & Company
PO Box 118
Bothell, WA 98041-0118 USA

1-800-426-3126
International: 1-425-483-3313
24-Hour Fax: 1-425-486-7596
Web site: www.patchwork.com
E-mail: info@martingale-pub.com

3/99

TUSCANY®

8 ” x 10 ”
(20 x 25 cm)

Silver Plate

Tarnish Resistant

DA VINCI LE COLLEZIONI®